# BECAUSE
# TOMORROW
## IS NOT
# PROMISED

# BECAUSE
# TOMORROW
## IS NOT
# PROMISED

*by*
Gene James, D. C.

BETTER HEALTH AND WELLNESS, INC
Phoenix, Arizona

Unless otherwise indicated, all scriptures are quoted from the *New International Version* of the bible, copyright 1973, 1978, 1984.

Cover design and typesetting by Jason Oxios

**Because Tomorrow is not Promised**
ISBN 0-9702823-0-3

Published by
BETTER HEALTH AND WELLNESS, INC.
1055 East Indian School Road
Phoenix, Arizona 85014-4811

Printed in the United States of America

# Contents

# Dedication

To all who have suffered losses, wrestled with disappointment and refuse to accept defeat. It is my hope that you will be encouraged and strengthened beyond measure.

To our nation and all who struggle to overcome the losses of September 11, 2001, keep the faith.

May God continue to bless America.

# Acknowledgements

First, I give thanks to God for giving me the breath of life and for breathing into me the inspiration to write these words.

To my wife, Kim, thank you for being who you are. You have always been my pillar of support.

Many thanks to Cheryl Garrison for working so patiently with me. Your editing brilliance has allowed this project to shine.

I am forever grateful to Eloise Miller, Annagail Lynnes and Jason Oxios for your invaluable assistance in allowing me to accomplish the dream of many and the reality of few.

# Introduction

*"Whenever I bring clouds over the earth and the rainbow appears in the clouds, I will remember my covenant between me and you."* (Genesis 9:14-15)

This book was written to declare the goodness and glory of God. It is my hope that you will be inspired along your journey. If you have ever cried out to God and did not get an answer, you will be encouraged. The bible refers to intervals of grief and pain as the "night season." This is a barren period where work ceases. As we toil, God reminds us that seasons are temporary. Jesus counsels us to carry out the work assigned us while it is day, because the night is coming when no one can work.

The passage, " whenever I bring clouds", tell us that God alone has the power to bring clouds into our lives, thus, if clouds exist in your life, God has purposed them. At times you may feel that you are alone in your suffering and no one understands. This is not so. As the verse continues, we find that God brings clouds "over the earth", which covers everyone. He causes his sun to rise on the evil and the good and sends rain on the righteous and the unrighteous. The trials that come into your life are no different from what others experience. The rain falls upon everyone.

The middle of the passage states "and the rainbow appears." Rainbows are present when the sun's rays are reflected through falling rain. In all of its beauty, a rainbow is only present when it rains. It becomes evident when the clouds pass and permit the sun to blend with the rain. We must allow the sunshine of God's presence to blend with our sorrow. When God sees the rainbow, He is reminded us of His promise to us. As His spirit is reflected throughout our lives, the rainbow appears and even our rainy days adorn us with beauty. God is looking for the rainbows.

## BE PREPARED

Time is filled with swift transitions. The rain came down, the streams rose, and the winds blew and beat against a certain house; yet it did not fall, because it had its foundation on the rock. Our survival during a storm is dependent upon the strength of our foundation. There is nothing that a season can bring that cannot be overcome with God.

## BE ENCOURAGED

As you read this book you should be reminded that everything happens in God's time. When the spies scouted out the Promised Land, the uproar that ensued upon their return was not about giants, it was about time. The Israelites did not realize what time it was. God assured them that despite the giants, obstacles, and their limitations, it was time. Likewise, the Hebrew boys were placed in the fiery furnace because it was time. God did not extinguish the flames; He simply joined them in the furnace. He did not remove Daniel from the lions' den; He changed the lions' nature from harm to harmony. When God is with us, flames cannot burn us, lions cannot devour us, giants will not destroy us and even death cannot keep our spirits down. God promises that He will never leave us nor forsake us. When we find ourselves in a den of despair we should not pray for God to move us; we should invite Him to join us. Because it's time.

Be encouraged. Along life's journey unexpected turbulence may arise and sudden storms may come your way but God has prepared a runway of peace. He is greater than any storm and He commands the rain. If you allow Him, He will be your comforter and guide. He is omniscient, omnipotent and omnipresent. He pardons the past and holds the future. He is God. If you already know Him, I hope that this book will give you a better understanding. If you do not know Him, I want to introduce Him to you.

# CHAPTER ONE

# A Time and a Season

## Points To Remember:

~Fear and doubt will challenge your faith~
~Extraordinary strength is revealed in extraordinary circumstances~
~A lifetime is not measured in months or years, but by precious moments~
~Regardless of who's in charge, God is always in control~

*"There is a time for everything, and a season for every activity under heaven:*
*a time to be born and a time to die, a time to weep and a time to laugh,*
*a time to mourn and a time to dance". (Ecclesiastes 3:1-2, 4)*

It was two a.m. on Christmas Eve. Kim woke me and didn't say anything. She just paced back and forth near our bed. She told me that she couldn't sleep because she was having contractions. Walking seemed to improve them, but they were becoming more intense. Up to this point her pregnancy had gone by the book. But babies don't read books; they come when they are ready. And this one was a few days early.

We felt somewhat prepared after attending the childbirth

classes, but we knew that anything could happen. The contractions seemed to be 18-20 minutes apart. This indicated that the birth was still some time away.

This was our first birth experience and we had decided to have our child at home. The birth method that we chose was the Bradley method, which is a husband coached childbirth process. My job was to comfort Kim during the birth experience by providing support and encouragement. This was done by recalling calming or pleasant experiences, massaging her back, encouraging her to breath and keeping her from becoming tense.

Kim appeared nervous and concerned, but she was calm. It is times like these that a person's true character is revealed. And she was cool under pressure. Much of the next few hours was spent with me coaching her through the contractions and accompanying her while she walked, sat, or layed down. I stayed with her the entire time.

At six o'clock that morning, her contractions were six minutes apart. It was time to call Pam, our midwife. She asked the usual questions that allowed her to assess Kim's progress. She told me that she would arrive shortly and to call if the contractions progressed.

About forty-five minutes later, Kim began to feel an overwhelming urge to push. Within minutes her water broke. I knew that the baby would soon be here. I called Pam and was told she had just left. She was still 20-25 minutes away. I didn't think that this baby had 20-25 minutes. It was ready to meet the world.

Kim continued to feel a compelling urge to push, as she got

into position for the delivery. My fear gave way to courage and I was no longer afraid. It was time to step up and do what had to be done. I remember feeling deep down that I could do this. What a joy it would be to deliver my own child.

I told her to push. And she did. I didn't want her to tear or overexert, so I cautioned her to slowdown, to pace herself. I must mention that at this point I was not sure what to do. As a coach it did not involve me having to go this far. I was acting merely on instinct. After a few more pushes the baby was crowning. During crowning, you can see and feel the top of the baby's head before it passes through the birth canal. I told Kim to rest for a moment and breathe because I knew that the next contraction would bring the baby out. After a brief rest, I gave her the command to push. She gave it all that she had and the baby came through with very little resistance. It was the highest high that I could imagine.

"Thank you, Jesus! Thank You, God!" It was truly a miracle. I moved the baby up to Kim's breast so that she could see her.

"Can you tell what it is?" she asked.

I checked her and told Kim excitedly, "It's a girl!"

"Khameela," Kim responded.

Khameela was the name that we had chosen for a girl and Ali was chosen for a boy. Then Kim asked me if the baby should be moving more or crying? I had never seen a newborn immediately after birth and I was not sure.

For the next few minutes we tried to get her to respond in some manner that would alleviate our concerns, but she only moved slightly. She was alive, but she was not responsive. We reasoned that she might be hungry so I moved her up to Kim's breast. Still, she did not respond. She was not active and she had a sort of bluish appearance. I recalled hearing that sometimes after birth it may take a few minutes for the baby to "pink up".

Time seemed to move slowly. A minute or so later our midwife arrived. She was excited to see that the baby had already come. She sounded very reassuring and we were relieved to see her. But when she took the baby into her arms, the look on her face said it all.

"This baby's not getting oxygen," she said. At once she began emergency procedures to revive her.

"Call 911!" was Pam's next order.

I was praying out loud to God, "Lord save this child, I know you can do it, help us Lord Jesus!" I made the call and it seemed that within minutes there were five paramedics in our bedroom. This birth experience that we had intended to keep private and intimate was out of control.

At some point during this crisis Kim began to have uncontrollable tremors. Her teeth began to chatter and she was jittery. But she still managed to maintain her composure during this very trying time. The paramedics evaluated Kim and assessed no signs of impending danger. She was administered an IV and was transported to the ambulance. I did all that I could do at that time; comfort Kim and pray.

The paramedics responded quickly to Khameela. Within minutes she was transported via helicopter to the hospital. Kim and I went by ambulance. I asked the paramedics if I could ride in the back with her, but was denied the request. This disappointed me because I had vowed to be with her through it all, for better or for worse, in sickness and in health. This type of interference was one of the primary reasons why we wanted to have our baby at home. I held her hand as they transported her to the ambulance. I felt numb and had mixed emotions ranging from fear, anger, frustration and guilt.

Pam told me that she would meet us at the hospital. I could see in her eyes how sorry she was, even though there was nothing that she could have done to change these events. As I was riding to the hospital I was thinking, "What now, Lord?" I felt totally unprepared because I thought that this was not supposed to happen. We had placed our faith in God's hands and it appeared that we were being punished. In some ways it seemed like a dream.

Upon arriving at the hospital, Kim appeared to be much improved. She asked me where they had taken Khameela and if we could go to her. She was not concerned with hospital protocol, admission procedures, or the IV that they were administering to her. She felt that her place was with Khameela. I've seen mothers shortly after delivery and they seem to be "out of it" for a day or so but Kim was definitely an exception.

Kim was taken to her room and the doctors began examining her. I took this opportunity to find out what I could about Khameela. The doctors and staff were performing tests to determine what had gone wrong. I went back to focus my attention on Kim. She asked me what they were doing. I told her I didn't know because they had not allowed me to see her.

Kim seemed to get stronger by the hour. She had always

been such a strong woman. I didn't know where her strength came from; it was as if she decided not to be a victim of circumstance.

"I want to take a shower," she said.

I began to help her up, but she was still connected to the IV. She put on a gown, took a few steps and looked at the IV.

"I don't need this," she said. She took the IV out and sat it on the table next to the bed. As we walked to the shower, it was obvious that Kim had overcome her circumstance and was not concerned with her condition anymore. She was walking without my assistance and was able to shower herself. After the shower, she wanted to see Khameela. I knew that this time nothing would stop her.

When we saw our baby, she was connected to an IV, breathing tube and monitors. She had become a medical case. We stayed with Khameela for some time, then we returned to Kim's room so that she could rest. I slept lightly that night and was attentive to Kim's needs. The following day was Christmas. The pediatric ward was festively decorated but it did little to offer comfort to us. Rather than pining over gifts, we sought answers and reassurance that things would work out all right.

The doctor's report concluded that Khameela had a congenital heart defect. They explained how the heart functions normally and the problems that Khameela was having. We did not believe them. We knew that as long as God existed, there was hope. And we began to pray and believe God would perform a miracle.

The doctor released Kim from the hospital that day. When

we returned home, I began calling a few friends and relatives to share our news and solicit their prayers. We slept and returned to the hospital in the afternoon. Intermittently doubt and guilt began to set in. I began to feel that God was punishing me for some past sin. I thought about the abortions that I had been associated with. Though I had never recommended an abortion, I did or said nothing to stop them. I repented and asked God for forgiveness. At times I could not believe that this was happening and tried to deny that it was. I even tried to bargain with God. "Lord, If you would spare her life, I will do whatever you want me to do." I even offered to preach the Gospel, which I felt was a calling on my life. I could feel God's presence. I felt desperate and helpless, but never alone.

*"I will never leave you nor forsake you."* Joshua 1:5

Kim was not interested in any of the details regarding Khameela. Even when the physicians made arrangements to give us their report of findings and discuss our options, she did not attend. I wasn't sure what was on her mind. But I think that she had already come to terms with our baby's fate, even though we both believed in miracles.

The following day was my birthday. The reality of Khameela's condition gave me little cause to celebrate. We arrived at the hospital early that day and as I met with the doctors, Kim visited Khameela. In their report, the doctors said that there was little hope for Khameela to have a normal life. The options were immediate surgery, wait weeks or months for a heart transplant, or remove her from life support. I knew immediately what had to be done, but I wanted to talk it over with Kim.

I found her standing next to Khameela's incubator. She had put booties on Khameela's feet and a cute little cap on her head. She told me excitedly that they allowed her to change Khameela. She said that her touch caused Khameela to raise her arms and feet. She even began to move around. It was obvious that Khameela knew when we were around.

I took Kim to one of the nearby nursing rooms to talk to her privately. I sat in front of her and held both of her hands in mine. I looked into her eyes, trying to maintain my composure, but I felt a rush of emotion. I wanted to get it out while I still could.

"She is real sick, Kim," I said, sobbing uncontrollably. We embraced and for the first time since the delivery, I was able to let my true emotions come forth. I wanted to get it all out so I did not try to stop crying. I looked up at Kim and noticed that she was not crying. I knew that she was feeling as much hurt as I was, but she denied herself this moment and instead chose to comfort me.

"We have to let her go," she said.

I knew what she meant and I agreed. We embraced one another in silence. We reserved commenting as we quietly accepted the will of God. I went to inform the doctors of our decision and Kim went to say goodbye to Khameela.

When I got back to the nursery they were taking Khameela off life support. They gave her to Kim. She held her for a moment and then gave her to me. She was so light. The doctor would check her heart every couple of minutes to see if there were any remaining signs of life. Then finally he looked up and told me, "she's in a much better place."

He handed her to me and Kim left. I could hear her crying softly as she walked away. Her mother was waiting at the end of the hallway. I sat down and talked to Khameela for a moment and rocked her in my arms. I felt that I was trying to wrap up a whole lifetime that we would have had together into that one moment. I don't remember feeling sad or angry. It was more like a feeling of peace as I recalled the doctor's words, "she's in a much better place."

Later the nurse came in and I carefully handed Khameela to her and left.

When Kim and I arrived home that night, it was quiet. I walked through the house, recalling the conversations that we had just one week earlier. We were anxiously counting down the days before there would be a new edition, complete with sleepless nights and diapers to change. Every room had some reminder of the new life that we expected. A changing table and diaper bag was in one bathroom; the other bathroom had baby oil, baby powder and pampers. There were toys scattered around our bedroom along with the many gifts that we received at the baby shower.

In the baby's room were more toys and the crib that still laid in wait. When I got back to the family room, I tried making light conversation with Kim. Our dialogue went back and forth talking about nothing. Definitely not talking about Khameela. I felt that we needed to do something, but what? I spotted a videotape that we had not watched. It was a tape from the 'Def Comedy Jam.' We had not seen the program and a friend had recorded six episodes. We agreed to watch it.

As we watched the video, we found ourselves laughing hysterically. We cuddled together on the floor and the pain that we felt gave way to power. Our laughter dried our tears and our faith began to heal our wounds. We praised God for bringing us through the storm and for not allowing our faith to fail us. Though we were just beginning our walk with God, our roots were deep enough in Him to allow us to weather the storm.

The bible says that, "weeping may endure for a night, But joy comes in the morning." Psalms 30:5.

Somewhere during the course of that evening, the morning came.

# CHAPTER TWO

# Joy Comes in the Morning

## Points To Remember:

~When grief is fresh the words should be few~
~Prayer turns pain into power~
~Faith will always move you forward~
~Those who sow in tears will reap in joy~

*"Come to me, all you who are weary and burdened, and I will give you rest.*
*Take my yoke upon you... For my yoke is easy and my burden is light."*
(Matthew 11:28)

If a structure is to withstand storms, it must be built with storms in mind. Our ability to recover from Khameela's death was subject to our preparation beforehand. So often we struggle with life's challenges with hope that tomorrow will bring healing. We believe that somehow it will be better in the morning. It is the strength of our foundation that allows us to endure overwhelming odds.

## Our Rock

During our time of sorrow, God was our rock. Kim and I began to view our experience as from the mountaintop rather than from the valley. The valley only permitted us to look up. The mountaintop allowed us to look over. We looked back over our lives and we could see from a distance where we had experienced exceeding joy and wonderful blessings. There were times of great fulfillment and tremendous favor. We reflected on how good God was and how far He had brought us. We never questioned God's judgment in good times and we felt unjustified to question Him during bad times. We concluded that we were blessed. What really mattered most during this trial was our relationship with each other and our relationship with God. And through it all He never left our side.

## Rise Up and Walk

One of the most remarkable recoveries I witnessed during our grieving period was watching Kim. She did not spend much time in sorrow. I remained close to her the next few days. Rather than comforting her, I was strengthened by her. There is no way of knowing how your mate will respond to perhaps the greatest trial that a parent can face, until it happens. Besides having to endure the loss of a child, she was also postpartum, which bears its own period of recovery. For the next few days there were numerous phone calls from family and friends expressing their sympathy and support. I witnessed Kim respond to each one with grace and unwavering faith. The following Sunday I addressed our church and conveyed our thanks for all those who offered their assistance, brought food, washed clothes and shared their love.

I could feel closure taking place within my spirit, though I purposely attempted to remain open. I did not want to simply file this experience away only to have it resurface in a more harmful manner. Kim and I spoke of Khameela often and I was free to discuss my feelings. God guided us through our grieving with the "peace that surpasses all understanding."

## Try Again

In no time, Kim was ready to try again. She asked me how long we should wait before trying to get pregnant again. Our midwife told us six weeks. I could tell that Kim was ready to move on. She asked how much time had passed. When I told her ten days, her response was, "is that all." I had a feeling that it was going to be a long six weeks.

After a few more weeks of waiting, we began trying. One of the funniest incidents occurred with the pregnancy test. We bought several of the home pregnancy tests and Kim anxiously tested herself every few days. After a few tries she came to me and asked if we were supposed to see a plus sign or two lines or something? I told her we should be getting some kind of sign.

"Well I'm not getting anything," she told me, "positive or negative." I went in to investigate. When I saw what she was doing, I broke out in laughter.

"Here, now try it," I told her, as I gave the test back to her. She had not removed the little plastic covering from the felt strip. She retook the test and confirmed what she already knew. Kim was pregnant.

### Well, If You Asked Me...

We could hardly wait to share the good news about the pregnancy. Many of our family and friends were waiting with great anticipation, as we were. Although for a few, their joy would turn into concern as they asked us if we were going to have this baby in a hospital. The truth was, given everything that we had experienced, Kim and I never considered a hospital birth. We were more determined than ever to have our baby at home. We knew that faith only moves forward. God has never given his people an option in matters of faith.

Those who thought that they had a right said, "well if you asked me..." But our response was, "no one asked you."

Faith is not something that you try for a season and then abandon if you obtain an unfavorable result. The bible says in Hebrews 10:38, "now the just shall live by faith; but if anyone draws back, My soul has no pleasure in him." Our faith was in forward motion

### I'm Scared

The next pregnancy went smoothly. Kim began to get a bit anxious as the due date approached but she was still in rare form. It is usual for the expectant mother to have an abundance of energy a day or so before the delivery date and Kim was no exception. On the eve of the birth, she told me that she wanted to buy a treadmill. So off we went to the fitness store. We did not know how close she was to delivering until she began testing the equipment they had in the store. The salesman was explaining the features of the treadmill Kim was demonstrating, when suddenly her water broke. I told the salesman, "we'll take this one." We left immediately.

We rushed home, which was not very far away, and began preparing for the birth. We went immediately into our relaxation and meditation as we had done before. Kim was calm and the preparation went smoothly. We called Pam and although the delivery was still several hours away, she came right over. In retrospect, we were all a bit tense during the labor. As Kim began pushing the baby through, she became hysterical.

"I'm scared, Gene," she screamed, "I'm scared."

"Everything's okay," I reassured her, "It's going to be all right!"

It seemed that was all she needed to hear, as she repeated the phrase softly, "it's going to be all right." Then as if her strength was renewed, she began to say to herself repeatedly, "just open up and let the baby out. Just open up and let the baby out. It's going to be all right. Just open up and let the baby out." And then she gave a big push. Pam tried to slow her down by telling her not to push so hard but Kim had waited a long time for this moment. The force of her push in some way reflected the struggle within her.

As we come to a familiar place, reminders of the painful past cause many to accept defeat or to not try. She refused to have an attitude of defeat and was strongly determined to have victory. Pam directed Kim to slow down but she was insistent. She pushed and pushed and our precious miracle came forth. With much joy and excitement we welcomed to our family Maya Adé James.

### Swift Transitions

Kim's fear emerged during the final stage of labor, just prior to the delivery. This period is called the transition. This is the shortest and most intense point of the birthing process. The contractions are continuous and relief cannot be found. It means that the delivery is imminent.

As you experience life's transitions, you will encounter your greatest challenges. Your endurance reaches its limit and your spirit becomes weak. A once manageable burden is at its most intense point and your strength fails you. You are at the point of "breakdown or breakthrough". Do not despair, your delivery is at hand. It is at this point that you must be still and allow God to move and be silent so that He can speak.

*"But those who wait on the Lord shall renew their strength; they shall mount up with wings like eagles, They shall run and not be weary, They shall walk and not faint".* (Isaiah 40:31 NKJV)

## Letting Go

After Khameela's death, we had bared our souls to God and allowed him to heal our wounded spirits. Our healing made us stronger and we had a greater appreciation for life. Releasing our pain brought joy and extended our own lives in the process. Kim and I have moved forward and have had three other children since Maya's birth. We were brought closer together through our experience and developed even greater faith in God.

Just as a tree produces its fruit in its season, our lives are also seasonal. The fruit of resentment and bitterness must fall to the ground and die, while the tree of hope remains. John 12:24 tell us, "unless a grain of wheat falls into the ground and dies, it remains alone; but if it dies, it produces much grain." A season comes when we, "let go and let God." When we render

20

authority to Him, He then commands the pain of the past to pass away. He will wipe away every tear from our eyes.

*"Those who sow in tears will reap in joy."* (Psalms 126:5)

## Take Time

Healing is sometimes a painful process. It takes time. Kim and I turned our pain into prayers and we began to sense God's presence and power. During a slow and painful recovery, many resort to counsel from man rather than council with God. They would rather have relief sooner than restoration. It is God's desire for us to draw nearer to Him during times of distress. He promises in His word that he would take our infirmities and bare our sicknesses. (Matthew 8:17)

Merely eliminating pain does not always promote healing; it oftentimes suspends the healing process. This evasive approach to life, where we avoid perceived painful experiences, will result in us becoming insensitive and unfeeling. We become incapable of expressing or receiving love, friendship or intimacy because of the risk involved. We must take the time necessary to complete our healing.

## Peace

Anger turned outward is danger and turned inward is pain. Separation from God because of anger leads us into rebellion and ends in pain. Anger and pain will never bring peace. If we desire true peace we must be reconciled with the Prince of Peace, our Lord and Savior, Jesus Christ.

An often asked questioned when enduring hardships is, "Why do bad things happen to good people?" The bible tells us clearly that "No one is good—except God alone." (Mark 10:18)

For all have sinned and fallen short of the glory of God. At the time of Khameela's death, Kim and I felt that we were living an exemplary life. We were attending church regularly and serving together in other capacities at our church. Then tragedy struck. Who do you turn to when you don't know whom to turn to? Where do you go when you don't know where to go? We sought answers in the word of God and were encouraged by learning a lesson from Job. If there was anyone who could really understand what we were going through, it was Job.

## BIBLICAL APPLICATION

Job was a man who was blameless and upright. He was the greatest man among all the people of the East. Even the Lord said to Satan, "there is no one on earth like him." (Job 1:8)

"Have you not put a hedge around him and his household and everything he has?" satan responded. "You have blessed the work of his hands, but stretch out your hand and strike everything he has, and he will surely curse you to your face."

God removed His hedge of protection from Job and his family, and in one day, Job experienced the worse tragedy imaginable. His seven sons and three daughters were feasting and drinking wine at their oldest brother's house when a mighty wind struck the house, collapsing it and killing them all. That same day Job lost all of his servants and livestock. Virtually all of his wealth was gone. How did Job respond?

Then he fell to the ground in worship and said: "Naked I came from my mother's womb, and naked I will depart. The Lord gave and the Lord has taken away; may the name of the Lord be praised." In all this, Job did not sin by charging God with wrongdoing. (Job 1:20-22)

Even at his worse Job continued to give God his best. His wife and close friends sat in judgment. They reasoned that Job was being punished for something that he had done and they suggested that he curse God and die. But Job knew that he had done nothing wrong. Oftentimes we may feel that death is the only relief for our pain. This is not true.

When God finally responded to Job he did not give him any answers. Instead He probed Job with questions. God asked, "Who is this that darkens my counsel with words without knowledge? Where were you when I laid the earth's foundation? Have you ever given orders to the morning, or shown the dawn its place? Have the gates of death been shown to you? Can you bring forth the constellations in their seasons or lead out the Bear with its cubs?"

Job could not begin to understand the forces that God had under his control. So often we try to envision God in our image rather than seeing ourselves in His. Job continued to believe in God despite his circumstances. He will ever be remembered for his faith and patience. At his lowest point, Job responded, "Though he slay me, yet will I trust in him." Job passed the test because he had an enduring spirit. He had faced the ultimate challenge. He lost his children, his property and his health. But he did not lose his most important possession, his faith.

After this, God made Job prosperous again and gave him twice as much as he had before. He lived an additional one hundred and forty years and saw his children and grandchildren to the fourth generation. The Lord blessed the latter part of Job's life more than the first.

Since Khameela's death, God has blessed us with four beautiful children, material possession and abundant health. Nothing can compare to what God has in store for those who love Him and faithfully keep his commandments.

# CHAPTER THREE

# A Lesson in Faith

## Points To Remember:

~Faith begins with believing and results in receiving~
~Faith must be combined with action~
~God may use us in our suffering so that others may understand and believe~
~Every miracle reveals a message~

*"If you do not stand firm in your faith, you will not stand at all".* (Isaiah 7:9)

One day I was looking for Kim and found her sitting and staring out the window. It was a particularly cloudy day, which seemed to have dampened her mood. I sat next to her and sensing her need for comfort, put my arms around her. After a moment of silence she said, "Khameela would have been a month old today." She began to weep. I refrained from commenting and instead held her close as she released her sorrow. Oftentimes our greatest expressions are unspoken. We embraced each other as we sat and gazed out the window. Words cannot heal a self-limiting condition; it must run its course. Kim and I knew that healing was a matter of time and faith.

## It Still Hurts

Those who have successfully undergone surgery know that the recovery can be painful. The danger is past but the pain is persistent. Following reconstructive surgery we may have to learn to walk or speak again. Deep emotional disturbance can also cripple us. Even though we come through it successfully, we may have to learn to love and live again. The experience may have left us weak and frightened but we can still be triumphant. Our victory proves that not only have we overcome our pain; we have overcome our past.

But why must it hurt? Pain prompts us to cry out to God but too often we simply choose to cry. When we cry out, we are yearning for comfort. When we cry, we are demanding relief. In our pain we still have free will. Why choose relief when God has promised to be our comforter and guide? God's comfort provides more than temporary ease of symptoms. It eases the pain of a broken heart.

## How Much Faith

The apostles said to Jesus, "Increase our faith."

The Lord responded, "If you have faith as a mustard seed, you can say to this mulberry tree, 'Be pulled up by the roots and be planted in the sea,' and it would obey you."

Jesus was in effect asking the apostles how much faith did they think they needed? It is not the measure of our faith that must grow. If we have only mustard seed faith, we can make things grow.

When we are hurting we focus on physical, mental and emotional healing, with little regard to healing the spirit. It is God's spirit within us that sustains life. When our spirits are broken we live broken lives, but we will live. Broken marriages, homes and dreams are a product of broken spirits. More people die each year from broken hearts than all of the medical conditions combined. When our spirits are lifted we have a reason to live. Our spirits are restored through prayer and applied faith.

## How Does Faith Work

*Everyone must submit himself to the governing authorities, for there is no authority except that which God has established. The authorities that exist have been established by God. Romans 13:1*

All existence operates under authority. Faith works because it abides under spiritual authority or laws. These laws were established by God; the law giver and law maker, since the beginning of time.

Spiritual principles are not logical from a sensory or physical standpoint. The laws are different. It's like hearing a foreign language for the first time. It does not make sense. This does not mean that what the speaker is saying is not logical. It simply means that it does not make sense, based upon your understanding. In the very same way, faith will not make sense if you operate in a physical world.

*By faith we understand that the universe was formed at God's command, so that what is seen was not made out of what was visible. Hebrews 11:3*

Everything began in the spirit realm. By faith God spoke everything into existence. The bible says that the earth was formless, empty and dark until God said, "let there be light," and there was light.

The world was created at God's command. In the spirit realm faith gives us the authority to command those things that we can not see. Health, prosperity, joy, peace... are at our spiritual command. Earlier, I used the example of a foreign language to illustrate that faith is not something that we can approach aimlessly. While visiting a foreign country you may discover that the laws and customs are different than those in your home land. Even your money may not be accepted as legal currency. If you wish to prosper in that land you must adhere to it's laws, customs and language.

In the spirit realm, the laws and customs are contained in the word of God (the bible). The language of the spirit is prayer and the accepted currency is faith.

*I tell you the truth, if you have faith and do not doubt, not only can you do what was done... If you believe, you will receive whatever you ask for in prayer.*

Matthew 21:21,22

*This is the confidence we have in approaching God: that if we ask anything according to his will, he hears us. And if we know that he hears us—whatever we ask—we know that we have what we asked of him.*

1 John 5:14,15

*And I will do whatever you ask in my name, so that the Son may bring glory to the Father. You may ask me for anything in my name, and I will do it.*

John 14:13,14

## Faith Comes by Hearing

I learned what faith was as a small boy growing up in the Mississippi delta. My mother and grandmother used to sing songs of faith that spoke of the love and joy of Jesus. Often, this was the first sound I heard when I woke up in the morning and the last sound I heard at night. I remember them singing, "Because He (Jesus) lives, I can face tomorrow." In those days mothers didn't work and fathers didn't play. My father came home too late and too tired to offer much time to his children. He worked sometimes seven days a week without sick days, sick leave or sick pay. If he didn't work, he didn't get paid. But by God's grace, we never missed a meal and God always provided. His job did not provide benefits and we did not have insurance, but God granted us assurance.

One of mama's favorite songs was "Blessed Assurance." She wouldn't always get the words right and what she couldn't remember she made up. She would sing, "Blessed assurance, Jesus is mine, O' what a forecast, clothes on the line."

When she got to the part that she knew she would come on real strong and sing,

"This is my story, this is my song.

Praising' my savior all the day long."

Sometimes mama would blend songs together. She would begin with "Amazing Grace" move through "I Need Thee Every Hour" and end with "Precious Lord." She drew strength from the only source that she had. That source was God.

There were times when mama used to get real sick. Even to this day no one knows what was wrong. We lived in the backwoods of a small town called Shaw, Mississippi and I remember one incident in particular. My mother did not seem to get better on this occasion but gradually grew worse. By nightfall there was an accompaniment of friends and neighbors in our home. Some were in the bedroom tending to her and others were outside the bedroom praying. They kept rushing in and out of her bedroom and talking among themselves. I didn't know how serious my mother's condition was but not long before, my grandmother had died. I was afraid that I might lose my mother. I was about eight years old and I didn't know what to do, so I began to pray. All I remember praying was, "Lord, please don't let my mama die." I must have prayed myself to sleep because that's all I remember about that evening. But *somewhere during the night,"*...God answered my prayer. When I went to bed that night she was sick but when I got up that morning my mother was fixing breakfast as if nothing had ever happened. To me it was a miracle. I felt that I had been touched by the hand of God.

We all have a story to tell and a song to sing. Our lives have been enriched by the people and events that have touched us along our journey. The sense of touch is perhaps the most powerful sense that God has given us. A touch can awaken and arouse. It can caution as well as comfort. It has a way of transcending barriers and transferring emotions. That is why when we are upset with someone we say, "don't touch me." Studies have shown that infants who were denied touching had a much higher incidence of sickness and crib death. When Khameela was in the hospital, the monitors would always show favorable responses when we touched her.

Oftentimes, healing is just a touch away. It takes courage to reach out to someone when we are hurting. Our pain might prompt us to blame rather than embrace. When we blame others for our sorrow we withdraw from him or her. When we blame ourselves we withdraw from everyone.

I closely felt God's presence in my life as a child, but over time I began to distance myself from Him. Khameela's death reminded me that God never leaves us, we leave Him. I felt the need to get closer to Him and to renew our relationship. I needed a fresh touch.

I began to read the bible daily, which has always been a source of comfort and strength for me. My study of the word of God has led me into the ministry. During this time, Kim took an interest in quilting, which became a passion and has evolved into a business. Everyone heals in his or her own time and in their own way.

## BIBLICAL APPLICATION

One of the greatest examples of a healing touch occurred with a woman who had an issue of blood for 12 years.

According to the scriptures, "She suffered many things of many physicians and did not get better but only grew worse." There are some ailments that physicians can't cure. There are a few observations about this story that I feel are worth mentioning. I am not certain why the author omitted these, possibly because we might lose the emphasis of the story. First of all, there is no mention of how she heard about Jesus. I would like to believe that some one knew of her suffering and told her of His goodness and grace. It was obvious that she was a determined woman, and upon hearing (faith comes by hearing) about Jesus, she believed that he could heal her. Secondly, there was no account given of her age, race, religious affiliation, marital status, or whether she was a sinner or saved. One conclusion can be drawn; she was determined to see Jesus.

*For she thought, "If I can just touch his robe, I will be healed."*

(Matthew 9:21)

### Keep the Faith

A determined faith can move mountains. It sees no barriers. Faith sometimes walks alone but it must walk. It stands against overwhelming odds but it must stand. Faith is not stationary and inactive; it demands that it be proven. The woman came up behind Jesus and touched his garment and immediately her bleeding stopped and she felt in her body that she was freed from her suffering. She acted upon her faith.

After she was healed the scripture tells us that Jesus "kept on looking around to see who had done it." The frightened woman, trembling at the realization of what had happened to her, came and fell at his feet and told him what she had done. And he said to her, "Daughter, your faith has made you well. Go in peace. You have been healed." (Mark 5:32)

This woman refused to be sick and shut-in and she declined being weak and shut out. She had the faith to keep dreaming and the courage to keep trying. As she made her way through the crowd, her sickness hindered her effort. But it did not hinder her expectation. She fully expected a miracle. She reasoned that if she could just get close enough to touch the hem of his garment she would be made whole. She didn't want Jesus to examine her, console her or listen to her story. She just wanted to touch.... When she touched his garment, it was so powerful that Jesus stopped in his tracks, turned and looked to find out who had touched him.

If you really want to move Jesus you can do it with applied faith. The scripture did not say that he glanced up to see who touched him. It says, "he kept on looking around to see who had done it." Jesus did not stop to speak with the woman to rebuke her; he wanted to acknowledge her. He wanted her to know and understand what had really happened. She had just experienced a miracle but Jesus was going to give her the message. The miracle recalls what happened; the message relates why it happened.

Although the woman was healed instantly when she touched Jesus, there was something different about her healing than the other miracles Jesus performed. It was different than when Jesus told the lepers to go and show themselves to the priest or when he told a blind man to go to the pool and wash. In those instances, Jesus spoke the words. But in this case the woman spoke the words. Proverbs 18:21 clearly states that life and death are in the power of the tongue. She remained silent in her suffering, which means she did not complain about her condition. When she chose to speak, she spoke words of faith. What makes this miracle so powerful, is that her faith resulted in a self-fulfilling prophecy. She had no right to be there, in keeping with biblical teachings. According to scripture, a woman with an issue of blood was unclean. But she was there…

We can take comfort in this woman's courage because we all have issues of some kind that make us unclean and unworthy. The scripture tells us that all have sinned and fallen short of the glory of God. But like this woman, we are saved by grace through faith.

The Jewish law forbade a man from touching a menstruating woman because she was ceremonially unclean. This may explain why she reasoned within herself that if she just touched the hem of his garment she would be made whole.

## No More Doctors

*The woman had suffered a great deal from many doctors through the years and spent everything she had to pay them, but she was no better. In fact, she was worse. (Mark 5:26)*

We often pay a great price to others for what God gives us freely. A songwriter wrote:

O' what peace we often forfeit,

O' what needless pain we bear,

all because we do not carry

everything to God in prayer.

Our faith can work for us, or against us. It depends on what we place our faith in. It was the woman's issue of blood that made her unclean. But it was her faith in Jesus that restored and cleansed her. We can come to Jesus just as we are. The people came bent, broken and bleeding and he healed them all. Jesus never focuses on our physical conditions; it is the condition of our faith that is of utmost importance.

It is also remarkable in this story that this woman was able to muster the faith necessary to complete her healing. One can conclude that within her faith was power that superseded her physical condition. Jesus' disciples did not understand what he meant when he asked, "Who touched my clothes?" His disciples said to him, "all this crowd is pressing around you. How can you ask, 'Who touched me?'" (Mark 5: 31)

There were others who could have touched Jesus that day, but because of their unbelief, they did not receive a miracle. Even Jesus' disciples misunderstood what Jesus meant. There were people on all sides and any one of them could have touched him. The disciples were talking about a physical touch, but Jesus was talking about a spiritual touch. If you really want to touch Jesus, you must touch him through your spirit. It is only through your spirit that you can pray the prayer of faith. Only through your spirit can you receive God's goodness. John 4:23 tells us, the true worshipers will worship the Father in spirit and truth, for they are the kind of worshipers the Father seeks. Those who are close to you may not understand what you're going through. They may see what's happening on the outside, but only God knows what's going on inside.

### What Do You Expect?

Jesus told his disciples, "someone deliberately touched me, for I felt healing power go out from me." When the woman realized that Jesus knew, she began to tremble and fell to her knees before him. The whole crowd heard her explain why she had touched him and that she had been immediately healed.

*"Daughter," he said to her, "your faith has made you well. Go in peace."*

(Luke 8:46)

What was this woman prepared to give for her healing? Everything! There were always two crowds that came out in those days. The ones who wanted to see Jesus and those who wanted to serve Him. For many of us, when it becomes more difficult for us to suffer than to serve, that is when we decide to serve.

The woman came to Jesus expecting a miracle and that is what she received. Being in the right place is only one part of the equation. She was not lucky. Faith is not an accident, it is deliberate and it will direct you.

What are you expecting from Jesus? What compels you to come to him? How much faith do you need in order to change your circumstance? One thing is of supreme importance, your faith will never exceed your hope or your expectation.

It is only faith in Jesus Christ that releases God's healing power. Just as this woman approached Jesus (unclean, unworthy and ashamed), she left restored, renewed and respected. The bible says that God "resists the proud, but gives grace to the humble." If we humble ourselves, God will exalt us.

Jesus knew that the woman had touched him but he wanted her to willingly identify herself. He wanted her to recognize that it was not the garment that healed her, it was her faith. The woman was justified through her suffering and became the subject of Jesus' teaching. Our suffering does not go unnoticed. God may use us in our suffering so that others may understand and believe. He knows who we are and when we are suffering. But he may be waiting for us to make our way to him and willingly identify ourselves. Kim and I knew that Jesus could heal us. His word declares that he was sent to heal the brokenhearted. (Luke 4:18) Like many others who endure grief, we had questions but we did not insist that having answers were essential to our recovery. Having faith means that anyone who comes after Jesus must already know that he is, he knows, he can and he will.

# CHAPTER FOUR

# Deliverance

### Points To Remember:

~Complete healing cannot occur until deliverance takes place~
~Symptoms are felt at the surface but originate from the source~
~The natural person sometimes suffers while the spirit person heals~
~The restoration of life is evidenced by the yielding of fruit~

*No discipline seems pleasant at the time, but painful. Later on, however, it produces a harvest of righteousness and peace for those who have been trained by it. (Hebrews 12:11)*

You have no doubt heard the phrase, "no pain, no gain." This implies that our growth results from pain. Whereas the recovery from physical pain requires rest; emotional pain requires restoration. We must restore ourselves to God and allow Him to remove our pain and delivers us. If you have not been delivered from your pain, it still exists somewhere within you. When pain is dormant, it does not mean that it is absent. We have a choice; remission or complete recovery.

*"lead us not into temptation, but deliver us from evil."* Matthew 6:13

The most reassuring news that a cancer patient can receive during a post-surgical consultation is hearing the doctor say that he was "able to get it all." This means that the cancer has not spread to other organs or tissues, and for all practical purposes the patient is cancer-free. God wants to set you free.

## Growth Spurts

Each new season in our lives cannot be ushered in until the things of the previous one is assorted and put away. As we grow older it becomes more difficult to stow the past. When winter or summer ended, my mother used to store our clothes until the season returned the following year. I waited eagerly to wear all of my favorites but to my surprise they no longer fit me. My growth during the year was so imperceptible that it was not evident to me until a measurement of some kind was in place.

Unless we uphold a standard of valuation for our lives, we can not determine if we are moving forward or backwards. Each year, we should strive to outgrow ourselves. Our hope should be to sort old ways and means of achievement and establish a new benchmark of excellence. In doing so, we will arrive at our subsequent season and discover what a difference a year can make.

## Good News! Bad News!

Two friends were discussing their love of baseball when one of them raised an interesting question. "Is there baseball in heaven?" They concluded that the one who died first would come back and let the other know. After some time one of them died. The other waited and waited and never heard from his friend. Then one night while he was sleeping he heard someone at the foot of his bed calling to him. "Hey, Joe," the voice said quietly. He woke up and it was his friend. "I've got some good news and I've got some bad news, Joe," his friend said.

"What's the good news," Joe asked?

"The good news is that there is baseball in heaven," replied his friend. Joe was excited and as he was about to speak his friend interrupted him saying, "I've got some bad news, Joe."

"What's the bad news?" Joe inquired.

His friend responded, "the bad news, Joe, is you're pitching this Sunday."

The good news is heaven awaits us. The bad news is we have to die before we can get there.

Everyone wants to go to heaven but no one wants to die. In some cultures, death is not perceived as a final resting-place. It is a transition.

Nicodemus, a member of the Jewish ruling council, came to Jesus at night because he was searching for answers. Jesus responded to him, "unless one is born again, he cannot see the kingdom of God." Jesus was speaking of a death of our old rebellious nature. There cannot be a rebirth without death. It is not possible for us to cling to our sinful nature and be renewed with Christ Jesus. Colossians 3:5-6 tells us, "therefore put to death your members which are on the earth: fornication, uncleanness, passion, evil desire, and covetousness, which is idolatry. Because of these things the wrath of God is coming upon the sons of disobedience." The word further warns, "put off all anger, wrath, malice, blasphemy and filthy language out of your mouth. You are to put on the new man who is renewed in knowledge according to the image of Him (Jesus) who created him."

"How can a man be born when he is old?" Nicodemus asked. Jesus answered saying "no one can enter the kingdom of God unless he is born of water and the Spirit. Flesh gives birth to flesh, but the Spirit gives birth to spirit." When you have been baptized with water and received the indwelling of the Holy Spirit, you are set free from all bondage. God hears our groaning and He eagerly desires to deliver us.

Deliverance is usually accompanied by pain and succeeded by joy. We pray at times for God to relieve us but we are challenged to endure. God desires to deliver us. Pain is a measure placed there by Him so that we could detect our need for Him. It alerts us to His presence.

### The Enemy Within

*It is not the natural children who are God's children, but it is the children of the promise who are regarded as Abraham's offspring. (Romans 9:8)*

The bible tells us about the two natures that dwell within us: the sinful nature and the spirit nature. And they oppose one another. The sinful nature seeks all things that are natural while the spirit nature seeks all things that are spiritual. Becoming a slave to one makes us free from the other. When we are committed to righteousness we are free from sin. Romans 8:8 states that those controlled by the sinful nature cannot please God.

The spirit nature desires the things of God and the sinful

nature desires the things of the world. When we become one in Christ, we are no longer part of the world. Those who submit to God's divine authority and direction are theocentric people. Theocentrics are God-centered. God is the center of their lives and they seek to do those things that are pleasing to Him.

Those who submit to any other authority are egocentric people. Egocentrics are self-centered. They favor self-pleasing rather than God-pleasing. They Edge God Out of the center and position themselves there. Their thoughts, words and deeds revolve around themselves. If we follow the majority or popular opinion without giving respect to God, we are egocentric rather than theocentric.

A common tendency when we want favor from God is to try to have the best of both worlds by shifting God in and out of the center as we see fit. When troubles come, we move God into the center and as they are resolved we move Him out. On Sunday mornings we shift Him back into the center and as soon as the worship service is over we move Him out again. God deems these people as being lukewarm. It is his desire that we are either hot or cold.

Joshua addressed the Israelites saying, "choose you this day whom ye will serve." The prophet Elijah also went before the people and said, "how long will you waver between two opinions? It does not matter what the rest of the world is doing, but as for me and my house, we will serve the Lord."

## Renewing Our Strength

Our strength is renewed when we bring our physical bodies under subjection of the spirit. When we are spiritually dominant we possess the power of transformation and rebirth. This is the beginning of true deliverance. Our lives are dearer to God as His Spirit governs us. Spiritual dominance adds God's blessing upon all that we do.

One of the most profound practices that demonstrate this power is fasting. It is most effective because of its spiritual significance. Fasting is regarded as a means of seeking divine favor and protection. Biblically it is most associated with confession, repentance, and sorrow. Physically it is a source of cleansing and regeneration. Regardless of one's belief, the power of fasting has been universally established.

Our flesh gives power to sin and makes us rebellious to the things of God. It is only through denying sin its pleasure that its power can be defeated. We are made free of the desires of the flesh by submitting ourselves to the Spirit. This must become a daily commitment. When God's work is manifested in our lives we begin to bear His fruit.

### The Evidence of Fruit

'For three years now I've been coming to look for fruit on this fig tree and haven't found any. Cut it down! Why should it use up the soil?' "Sir," the man replied, "leave it alone for one more year, and I'll dig around it and fertilize it. If it bears fruit next year, fine! If not, then cut it down."

(Luke 13: 7-9)

God intends for us to bear fruit. His first command to Adam and Eve after he blessed them was to be fruitful and multiply. Material possessions and prosperous living do not evidence fruitful lives. In reference to the parable, we are like the fig tree. For years, many of us have been coming to the house of God and prospering in His vineyard but not bearing His fruit. We may have the misplaced notion that if we are prosperous then we are favored. The truth is we are not prospering because of God's favor but because of His grace and mercy.

The justice that we deserve is to be cut down and thrown into the fire. But we are saved by His grace through faith. When we have said yes to everyone and everything except God, it is God's grace and mercy that intercedes on our behalf and bids us more time

Sadly, many do not understand the hedge of protection that they have been afforded. And they fail to realize that they only have limited coverage. Their policy has an expiration date and when it expires, they expire. It can only be renewed through the blood covenant of Jesus Christ.

## Spiritual Fruit

*He shall be like a tree planted by the rivers of water, That brings forth its fruit in its season, Whose leaf also shall not wither; And whatever he does shall prosper.* (Psalms 1:3 NKJV)

Those who are led by God's Spirit will yield the fruit of the spirit. The Spirit produces love, joy, peace, patience, kindness, goodness, faithfulness, gentleness and self-control.

Again, God's word likens us to a tree. In order for a tree to produce fruit it must first remain planted. Each time it is uprooted, it must become rooted in its new environment before fruit bearing results. Very often we are not bearing fruit in our lives because we are not remaining rooted long enough. Just because the world is constantly changing does not mean that we have to. Uprooting ourselves in an untimely manner does not result in immediate fruit. Sometimes our impatience causes us to miss a season.

In our effort to bear spiritual fruit we must remain rooted in the word of God and allow Him to enter our hearts and nourish the roots of our souls. We are to immerse ourselves in God's Word until our fruit-bearing season comes. As we persevere we are to reflect actions and attitudes that honor God.

Just as a tree cannot benefit from its own fruit, the fruit that we produce (love, peace, joy, etc.) is for others to partake. We must release it freely so that we may reap a greater harvest in subsequent seasons. God promises us many seasons in our lives and each season brings challenges and blessings. If a tree selfishly clings to fruit that it cannot use, it ceases to prosper, its leaves begin to wither and it can die. Many are withering and dying because they are not releasing their fruit.

### The Greatest Fruit

*If I give all I possess to the poor and surrender my body to the flames, but have not love, I gain nothing. (1 Corinthians 13:3)*

This scripture implies that it is possible to give without loving. But John 3:16 suggests that we cannot love without giving. "For God so loved the world that he gave his one and only Son, that whoever believes in him shall not perish but have eternal life." True love is unselfish and unconditional. It is the greatest of the spiritual fruit.

Unselfish fruit possesses unselfish seeds. Each seed holds the promise that if planted it will reproduce an abundance of fruit of its own kind. When we love someone without restrictions, we sow a seed of love into that person's life. This seed can create for him or her a harvest of love, season after season. Once we have received the genuine article, our lives are transcended to a higher dimension and a new standard of love is established.

The greatest example of love is God's love for us and Christ's love for his church. If we could accept the love that God freely gives us it would change our lives. Many of us are less likely to accept unconditional love because we will not accept that which we are unwilling to give. Love does not obligate us; it frees us. The love of God is not a reciprocating love that requires love first before it is returned. This is not true love. God's love is directed outward while reciprocating love is directed inward.

## BIBLICAL APPLICATION

We are often removed from the well-trodden path as we push toward our destiny. God told Abram to leave his country, people and father's household and go to a land that God would show him. Jacob and Joseph were also led away from the comfort of their father's home to a pre-destined place. Jacob left his family and went to a strange land before he could find his destiny, his wife and himself. As we follow God, we must be prepared for Him to move us.

Too often we manage our lives with indifference to the will of God. He is not pleased when we consent to relationships and circumstances that profit us but do not glorify Him. If we want to receive the promises of God we must relinquish control to Him.

Like many of us, Jacob learned to surrender and trust God.

The first stage of his life was filled with deceit. His environment and the influences on his life would not allow him to commit completely to God. He had deceived his brother out of his birthright and with his mother's help, stole his brother's blessing. He had to be purged and made into the man that God could use.

## Deliverance from the Past

During the second stage of Jacob's life, the tables turned and his uncle Laban deceived him. He was forced to work fourteen years to pay off a seven-year debt and his wages were changed ten times. After a fourteen-year gestation period, he could finally receive what God had for him. Jacob worked an additional six years after his debt had been paid before he left. He was waiting on God.

We will face our past over and over until we either submit to or overcome it. Perhaps during this period of adjustment Jacob had time to reflect on the promise that God had made to him and he began to feel God at work in his life. Like Jacob, so many of us have to resist taking matters into our own hands. Holding steadfast and trusting God requires great courage.

## Deliverance from Bondage

The first time the Lord appeared to Jacob was in a dream. He was fleeing from his brother Esau and sought refuge with his uncle Laban. God renewed his covenant with Jacob and made a promise to him saying, "I am with you and will watch over you wherever you go, and I will bring you back to this land. I will not leave you until I have done what I have promised you." (Genesis 28:15)

The second time Jacob encountered angels, he was again in flight. This time he was fleeing from his uncle Laban. He was also preparing to face his brother Esau, who he had deceived twenty years earlier. He was afraid. The presence of the angels confirmed for Jacob that God was still with him. He was forced to face his past as he was running from his present.

During times of strong opposition, we must stop to acknowledge God's presence in our lives and be encouraged that He is still with us. Jacob's next encounter with God was when he had to face Esau. At this point it appeared that Jacob was tired of running. He realized that there was something inside of him that had to be delivered.

The night before he was to meet his brother Esau, Jacob seemed determined to break the curse upon his life. He sent his family and possessions across the Jabbok River while he was left alone in the camp. Jacob wrestled with a man until daybreak and refused to let go until the man blessed him. He knew that when it was all over, there was a blessing in store for him. When the man saw that he could not overpower Jacob, he touched the socket of Jacob's hip so that his hip was wrenched as they wrestled. Jacob endured pain, but he did not let go.

The man asked him, "What is your name?" "Jacob," he answered. Then the man said, "Your name will no longer be Jacob, but Israel, because you have struggled with God and with men and have overcome." (Genesis 32:27-28)

Somewhere beyond the conditions, problems and uncertainties that we are wrestling with is our blessing. The source of our problems can rarely be managed by examining the surface.

Symptoms are only the manifestation of deeper problems. In the same way that a fire cannot be extinguished by removing the smoke detector; removing the symptoms cannot solve problems. We must go deeper and acquire the fire.

## I Still Don't Get It

I never understood some of the things that my parents tried to teach me when I was a child. I had to experience them as an adult. Thus, a lack of understanding or stubbornness on my part forced me to learn some lessons the hard way.

At our previous home, Kim and I would occasionally rescue an animal that had come down from the mountains to drink from our pool. Some would fall in accidentally while drinking, others would get in purposely, only to discover that they could not get out. Sometimes we got to them in time to save them. Othertimes we were too late. Driven by their thirst, these animals welcomed themselves into something that offered them no way out. Those that were rescued in time experienced true deliverance.

When God answers your prayer and delivers you, you will experience renewed joy and restored passion. Old things will have passed away and all things will become new again. Howard E. Smith wrote:

I was sinking deep in sin, Far from the peaceful shore,
Very deeply stained within, Sinking to rise no more;
But the Master of the sea heard my despairing cry,
From the waters lifted me- now safe am I.

# CHAPTER FIVE

# From This Day Forth

## Points To Remember:

~There are no perfect people, hence no perfect marriages~
~Unless the Lord builds the house, its builders labor in vain~
~Big ships can't come too close to the shore~
~Perfect love casts out all fear~

*The Lord God said, "It is not good for the man to be alone. I will make a helper suitable for him." (Genesis 2:18)*

The union between a husband and wife is tested during hardships. Adversity can draw them closer together or push them further apart. The bible tells us that a man will leave his father and mother and be united to his wife, and they will become one flesh. One flesh means that neither should bear their cross alone. We are also charged to submit to one another. Godly submission does not mean that we are subordinate, secondary or inferior. It means that we are strong enough to be weak and exalted enough to be humble.

As I mentioned previously, when I revealed Khameela's condition to Kim I wept inconsolably. I humbled myself before her and she submitted herself to me. She was comforter and nurturer. Woman was given to man to be a helpmeet, who is a companion and helper. The goal of every marriage should be oneness, with neither being complete without the other. This is more than seeking someone whom you can live with; it is holding out for someone whom you can't live without.

## Drop Everything and Go

When I first met Kim, I almost blew it. I was a vendor positioned among the many others that attended the Black Women's Task Force conference one year. Most of the day was fairly uneventful, except between sessions where there would be a rush of traffic for a brief moment and then little activity in between. Kim passed by my booth among the crowd and immediately caught my eye. She seemed disinterested in the exhibits. In fact, she was some distance away as she passed by.

After she passed, a little voice told me to go after her. In a flash, I left my post and went after Kim, but I could not find her. She was now lost in the crowd. I returned to my booth and waited. When I saw her passing by the opposite direction (again from a distance) I was determined to get her attention. I called her over and as she approached the booth, she recognized my office manager. They were members of the same sorority, Alpha Kappa Alpha. They began to reminisce and renew their friendship but I was in no rush. I knew that my ship had come in.

There was something special about her and I was determined to find out what it was. We exchanged glances and light conversation. I knew that it was not the last time that I would see her. Finally, she exchanged phone numbers with my office manager and left. Afterwards my office manager asked me, "what did you think?" I did not have to think, I knew. You don't meet someone like that everyday. She began to tell me that she would call her to find out if Kim had a boyfriend. I interrupted, "it doesn't matter if she has a boyfriend, he's got to go." I wasn't interested in who he was or where he was going, I just knew that he had to leave. I had never reacted that way about anyone prior to meeting Kim. I knew our meeting was destined for that time.

## Waiting For Your Ship to Come In

Kim and I have discussed the events of that day on several occasions and I will share with you the lessons that I learned. The first is we never know how or when God will bless us. We must remain open and prepared. Secondly, even when God gives to us, we are still required to take some action of faith to receive it. Thirdly, trust your heart and don't allow logic or understanding to block your blessing. While I was going through deduction, induction and reasoning, Kim was gone.

I've learned that when cruise ships go to port on some remote locations they will drop anchor some distance away from the island and the passengers must take small charters to shore. It never dawned on me why they did this until I went on a cruise. It is the same reason why Kim did not pass by in close proximity to me. Big ships can't come too close to the shore. The water is to shallow.

If you want to get to your ship you have to leave the shore of shallow thinking and launch out into the deep ocean of faith and destiny. Like two ships passing in the night, Kim passed by from a distance on both occasions. I almost blew it because my shallow thinking was; "if God has someone for me then it would be easy."

When she passed by the first time, that was my predominant thought but I received a quick revelation when I could not find her. But I am so glad that God gives us second chances. When she returned, I left my booth; the same way that the followers of Jesus did when he said follow me. God's provisions for us require that we deny ourselves, accept the challenge and step out on faith.

*"Come, follow me," Jesus said, "and I will make you fishers of men." At once*
*they left their nets and followed him.* (Matthew 4:19-20)

### Set Our Sails

Why do we so often assume that if something is for us, it must be easy? Many of the things that I have enjoyed, I have had to work at them and grow until God saw me worthy to receive them. Every relationship that I had prior to meeting Kim was necessary for me to become the person that could accept and appreciate her. I had to learn and grow from each one. Too often we place conditions on how God should bless us. God never promised us that the road would be easy.

When asked why he wanted to run for president, Rev. Jesse Jackson responded:
"I'm tired of sailing my little boat
so far inside the harbor bar;
I want to go out where the big ships float
out on the deep where the great ones are.
And should my frail craft seem too slight

and the waves would sweep my billows o'er
I'd rather go down in a stirring fight
than drown to death at the sheltered shore."
1988 National Democratic Convention

## Worth Waiting For

The bible gives the account of Jacob who wanted Rachel as his wife but he had to work seven years before he could have her. True love is worth the wait and will make you wait. It can be distinguished from lust because lust demands immediate gratification. When I met Kim, I wanted to take the time and get to know her. As it was done in the "old days."

I met a couple while I worked in Inglewood, California that taught me a lesson in love. Carmen and Jerry were high school sweethearts who dreamed of living their lives together. While in his senior year of high school, Jerry made a promise to Carmen. He said that he "would love her forever," and some day he would marry her. This promise was sealed with a kiss and he gave her a ring as a symbol of his love. Jerry received a music scholarship at a large midwestern university and while he was there, he started to play for a local band to earn extra money. As a result, he experienced a great deal of recognition; as well as much attention from the campus co-eds. He remembered his promise to Carmen and remained faithful, until one night, when the unthinkable occurred.

After a late-night gig he accepted the offer from Grace, a friend, to stay with her and return to the campus the next morning. As a result of this moment of passion, Grace became pregnant. Jerry's parents raised him with a deep respect for others and he knew that he would not disgrace her. The only respectable thing to do was to marry her. Carmen was hurt, but she knew Jerry. And she found it in her heart to forgive him. Jerry and Grace were married and had three children. After fifty years together, Grace died.

Several years later, Jerry was visiting his hometown and inquired about Carmen, who unknown to him had recently retired and moved back to the area. He decided to call her. She recognized his voice immediately and was delighted to hear from him. They had not spoken for over fifty years because he thought that she had never forgiven him. He was surprised to find that she had never married. She told him that she was engaged a few times but it never seemed right. They arranged a meeting and afterwards they promised to keep in touch. Six months later they were married. He was 73 and she was 71.

"The splendor of love is that it has no bounds but the glory of love is that its power is everlasting."

## Do You Know This Man

I am amazed at the number of people who have gotten married and did not really know the person they married. It is so easy to become obsessed with planning the wedding that we neglect to make plans for the marriage. We are brides and grooms for a brief moment, but husbands and wives for a lifetime. In preparation for a wedding, we meticulously consider every detail, such as the invitations, music, budget, location, rehearsals, etc. All of these essentials are well thought-out for an event that lasts one day. But many times little consideration is given to the day after.

Statistically, one-in-four marriages will not survive the first year. The reason given is "irreconcilable differences". I have heard arguments from both sides of this issue and I can only conclude that they made a poor choice.

*"Unless the Lord builds the house, its builders labor in vain."* (Psalms 127:1)

## Getting To Know You

After we began dating, Kim and I spent a lot of time talking. Our conversations would continue until two or three o'clock in the morning and on one occasion until sunrise. Our topics of discussion varied from intimate and personal to superficial and free. Kim was and still is the most candid and giving person that I have met.

When the queen of Sheba heard about the fame of King Solomon and his relation to the name of the Lord, she came to test him with hard questions. He far exceeded her expectations in both wisdom and wealth. The bible says that she was left, breathless. My early relationship with Kim was very much the same. I asked lots of questions, which she answered without hesitation. I resolved that when God's hand is upon a relationship or person not only will they withstand the test of time, they will withstand any test that you put before them.

It is important to learn as much as possible about our mates before we are married. There are no perfect people. We all fall short in some area of our lives. An openness and desire to communicate with each other strengthens our relationships. It is a common weakness to favor relationships and activities that do not challenge us to open up and venture away from the shore. Being open means that we humble ourselves. We purge our pride by baring our weaknesses. Openness sheds the exterior wall and allows our true essence to be revealed.

## Leave the Shore

When Kim and I were in Hawaii for our honeymoon, we visited every island. We saw all that we could in the time allowed and did all that we could find to do. I was glad that we shared so many interests and activities. Before we arrived in Hawaii we discussed some of the things that we would do. Even after we arrived, we made daily plans. Our honeymoon would not have been as much fun without effective communication.

We have had conversations with other couples who had gone to Hawaii and sat at the beach everyday. Kim and I went on sunset cruises, snorkeling, jet skiing and luaus. They went to the beach, went shopping and back to the hotel. Another couple didn't discuss any details of their honeymoon prior to getting married. As the wedding date approached the bride-to-be asked her fiancé where they were going and he told her that it was going to be a surprise. The surprise was two days and one night at a nearby timeshare location where they had to attend a two hour sales presentation. I must admit that being in Hawaii and sitting on the beach would have been much more fun than attending a timeshare presentation on your honeymoon.

Relationships that lack deep physical intimacy usually lack emotional intimacy. Deep intimacy comes from thought provoking and absorbing communication. If our conversation stems from shallow and frivolous issues we will have shallow a relationship.

## God made us Different

It has been said that if two people agree on everything, one of them is not necessary. God made us different for a purpose and if we cannot appreciate the difference, we should review our purpose. One person may be winter and summer while the other is spring and fall. We need all seasons. One is strength and the other is heart. One is warm, the other cool. We must learn to be still and allow God's purpose, his perfect plan for us and the person in our life to be revealed.

Inevitably problems will result. When confronted with differences of opinion, it is important to find the right time and the right tone to discuss them. In some relationships uncertainty seem to result more from our indifferences than differences. Couples who are indifferent toward one another lack emotional involvement and show little interest or regard for each other's welfare. This neutral or detached character trait implies selfishness and hinders effective communication and growth. Disagreements should be discussed and resolved quickly. The key is to defer our emotions while resolving emotional issues.

## BIBLICAL APPLICATION

*And in him (Christ Jesus) you too are being built together to become a dwelling in which God lives by his Spirit. (Ephesians 2:22)*

One of the first places that Kim and I went together was to church. This was a first for me. I believed in separation of church and relationships. Building a strong relationship is much like building a house, where God is the master architect and builder. We brought our ideas and desires to the architect and He prepared the plans for our relationship and marriage. As with any building process, our relationship has also undergone different phases of construction. Our marriage's ability to withstand strong forces has been predicated upon the foundation that it was built. That foundation is God.

The ancient Egyptians knew the importance of a solid foundation. Their architecture still defies modern science because it has endured the test of time. It still stands because God inspired it. Their skills were God-given. When we allow God to inspire our relationships and marriages, they will defy the odds. A God-based relationship will have strength and commonground because a threefold cord (God, husband and wife) is not easily broken.

Marriage is a holy institution ordained by God. In Genesis 2:18 the Lord God said, "it is not good that man should be alone; I will make a helper comparable to him." It further states that God formed the beasts, birds and every living creature and brought them unto Adam to name them but there was not found a helper comparable to him. The first point that this scripture makes is that God is not pleased with the solitude of man. He said that it is not good that man should be alone. God did not simply state that it was not good that Adam should be alone because He knew that everything that affected Adam would consequently affect mankind. Then God was determined to make a helper that would be comparable to Adam. We often seek those who are compatible with us. Our desire for compatibility is to find someone who is in agreement with us or one who is adaptable to ourselves. But God sought a helper who was comparable to man. Those who are comparable with us share similar likeness and are equivalent to us in every way.

He caused Adam to fall into a deep sleep; and while he was sleeping, God took one of Adam's ribs and made woman (men have loved ribs ever since). God caused the sleep to fall upon Adam because if Adam had been awake he might have tried to interfere with the work of God. He might have tried to tell God how to do His work. In the latter part of verse 22 it states, "He (God) brought her to the man." Based upon this scripture many believers are waiting for God to bring them a mate. But in the former part of this verse it tells us that God took the rib from the man and made woman. The conclusion is, God did not bring the woman to Adam; he brought her from him. In doing so, the woman was not greater or less than Adam, she was him. We may ask God to bring us the right or ideal mate but we must bear in mind that God will not have us unequally yoked.

James 1:17 tells us that every good and perfect gift is from above. If we cannot bear perfection, we will not receive it. We must show ourselves worthy to receive the gifts that God has for us. He further informs us to be perfect and complete, lacking nothing. When we give our best, it is returned in good measure, pressed down, shaken together and running over. In summary, the best will not come to us until it originates from us.

# CHAPTER SIX

# Prayer Changes Things

## Points To Remember:

~God answers every prayer in his own way and in His own time~
~Prayer changes things but praise changes people~
~Our prayers should express our desires, but we should accept God's will~
~God remembers those who have been faithful to Him~

*Without warning, a furious storm came up on the lake, so that the waves swept over the boat. But Jesus was sleeping... (Matthew 8:24)*

While Kim and I were returning home from our honeymoon in Hawaii we experienced the worst turbulence imaginable. The plane felt like it was being torn apart. We watched as the flight attendants tried to attend to their duties as usual. They were being tossed about the cabin by the storm. We anxiously waited for the captain to tell us something that would reassure us that all was well, but we didn't hear from him.

The crew continued to carry on the facade. Finally, they started whispering to each other. Kim and I overheard, "He wants us to sit down, right now." They looked concerned. We were concerned from the start. Still, we heard no word from the captain.

Suddenly, the plane dipped violently and one of the flight attendants literally struck her head on the ceiling. At that time, I knew that we were in danger. Desert Storm had just begun the previous week and we felt like we were in the midst of it. This continued for nearly an hour. The plane shifted, swayed, dipped, pitched and finally began to settle down for the rest of the flight.

As I look back on that day, I was afraid. We were all afraid. We needed to hear a word from the captain and never heard from him. So often we go through turbulent times and we are waiting to hear from God and it seems that we never get a response. "Lord, give us some kind of assurance that what we're going through is only temporary, that it's only turbulence." Inside our plane that day were hundreds of people of all races, religions, first class, coach, sinner and saved. But regardless of our differences, we had one single concern: Help us make it through the storm. When we landed, everyone had felt the power of God and the helplessness of man. The captain fought valiantly to maintain control of the plane, but it was our heavenly captain who landed us safely that day. God is the only one that we can rely on through the storm.

## When It's All Over

I am certain that everyone on our plane was praying that day. Jesus told us where two or three are gathered together in His name, He is there in the midst of them. Our gathering was by chance, not by choice, and God used this chance to bring about change. Lives were changed that day.

Some of the circumstances that we endure in our lives are intended to bring about change. At times, our blessings come after our change comes. We pray for help and God extends His hand. He invites us to seek refuge in Him. He says, come to me, all you who are weary and burdened, and I will give you rest. (Matthew 11:28)

The bible instructs us to be anxious (or worry) for nothing, but in everything by prayer and supplication, with thanksgiving, let our requests be made known to God. If we have time to worry; we have time to pray. We should convert worrying time into praying time. During periods of troubles, our prayers often become selfish or petition prayers. Prayer should be coupled with thanksgiving and praise.

## BIBLICAL APPLICATION

On His way to Jerusalem, ten men who had leprosy met Jesus. They stood at a distance and called out in a loud voice, "Jesus, Master, have mercy on us!" When he saw them, he said, "Go, show yourselves to the priests." And as they went, they were cleansed. One of them, when he saw he was healed, came back praising God in a loud voice.

The lepers story began with them pleading for mercy. It ended with the impartation of grace. The fairness of their condition demanded that they suffer but they believed that Jesus had the power to pardon them and grant their freedom. The scripture states that while they were walking they were cleansed of their leprosy. They were moved from mercy to grace through their faith. It was their faith that healed them but their healing was not completed until they began walking. We are saved by grace through faith.

Without faith it is impossible to please God. So often He has approved our healing but it is not completed until we begin walking in faith. When we pray a prayer of faith, believing that we have received that which we have asked, we should get up off our knees and begin preparing a place for our blessing. Of the ten lepers only one returned to Jesus. Faith sent him away but praise brought him back.

## Our Father

Jesus' disciples asked him to teach them to pray and he taught them in this manner. Our Father in heaven. The opening of this model prayer suggests that it is an intercessory prayer. Our Father implies that we are either praying with or for someone. There is no reference to I, me, my and mine but we, us and ours. Give us, forgive us, lead us and deliver us, are the examples.

## Hallowed Be Your Name

That which is hallowed is set apart for sacred and holy worship. We are declaring in our prayers that God's name only is holy. Sincere prayer is more than just words. If our prayers are to be effective, they must be fervent and righteous. We cannot pray righteous prayers if we live unrighteous lives. When we expect God to bless us in our unrighteousness we are in effect bringing Him clean hands but dirty hearts.

## Your Will Be Done

King Hezekiah was a man whose heart was right with God.

The scriptures tell us that he trusted in God, kept his commands and did not cease to follow him. The Lord was with him and made him successful in whatever he undertook. One day Hezekiah became ill and was at the point of death and the Lord sent the prophet Isaiah to him. His message was simple, "put your house in order, because you are going to die." Upon hearing the news, Hezekiah turned his face to the wall and prayed to the Lord. "Remember, O Lord, how I have walked before you faithfully and with wholehearted devotion and have done what is good in your eyes." And Hezekiah wept bitterly.

Hezekiah did not lie prostrate on the floor and beg for healing or for a longer life span. He prayed that God would remember the things that he had done and count him faithful. Hezekiah accepted the will of God.

Before Isaiah left the middle court, the word of the Lord came to him telling him to "go back and tell Hezekiah, the leader of my people, 'This is what the Lord, the God of your father David, says: I have heard your prayer and seen your tears; I will heal you. On the third day from now you will go up to the temple of the Lord. I will add fifteen years to your life." (II Kings 20:4-6)

## Give Us This Day

This is an all too familiar phrase that is commonly recited in our prayers. Do we ever stop to realize it's meaning?

*"Keep falsehood and lies far from me; give me neither poverty nor riches, but give me only my daily bread. Otherwise, I may have too much and disown you and say, 'Who is the Lord?' Or I may become poor and steal, and so dishonor the name of my God." (Proverb 30:8-9)*

We ask God to give us what is sufficient for the day. Not so much that we can brag and disown Him or so little that we will steal and dishonor Him.

As the Israelites marched through the wilderness they became hungry. God provided for them manna from heaven. They were to gather enough for the day. The manna was meant to provide for their immediate needs on their journey to the promised land. If they had received anything more, they might have become content and given up their journey. Sometimes we must remain hungry while we are working toward our prize. Too often we become content with manna. We settle for what is present and forsake what is promised.

## As We Forgive

We are asking God to apply the same degree of mercy upon us as we apply to others. In the sermon on the mount, Jesus taught; blessed are the merciful, for they shall obtain mercy. This is part of the standard of conduct for believers. If we want to be blessed, bless others. God cannot loose our request from heaven until we loose them on earth. We cannot ask God to loose mercy, forgiveness and peace from heaven if we're binding them on earth. Forgiveness means that we are holding hands and not holding grudges.

## Lead Us Not Into Temptation

*When tempted, no one should say, God is tempting me… but each one is tempted when, by his own evil desire, he is dragged away and enticed. Then, after desire has conceived, it gives birth to sin; and sin, when it is full-grown, gives birth to death. (James 1:13-15)*

We should pray daily that God would direct us away from

temptation, which lures us from his presence. Our desires lead us into temptation. We cannot be tempted with that which we do not desire. How do we resist temptation? By changing our desires. How do we change our desires? By changing our environment. Our desire leads to temptation, which precedes sin, and results in death.

In Paul's first letter to Timothy he counselled that people who wanted to get rich fell into temptation and harmful desires that plunged them into ruin and destruction. "For the love of money is a root of all kinds of evil." (I Timothy 6:10) Some people, eager for money, had wandered from the faith, which resulted in much grief.

Exposure to God changes us by allowing new experiences. Our experiences with God influence our thinking, and as the bible says, "For as he thinks in his heart, so is he". (Proverbs 23:7) Our actions do not determine who we are. Who we are is the summary of our thoughts.

## Thine Is the Power and The Glory

Our battles and victories are not personal. God shares them with us and He should receive glory in both. Any attempts to steal God's glory, forfeits our reward. We are not paid on commission, but on the Great Commission. We will receive our ultimate reward in glory. Matthew 6 tells us, "when you do a charitable deed, do not sound a trumpet before you as the hypocrites do in the synagogues and in the streets, that they may have glory from men. Assuredly, I say to you, they have their reward. But when you do a charitable deed, do not let your left hand know what your right hand is doing, that your charitable deed may be in secret; and your Father who sees in secret will Himself reward you openly."

On one occasion King Herod addressed the people of Tyre and Sidon and upon his completion the people shouted, "this is the voice of a god, not a man." Immediately, because Herod did not give praise to God, an angel of the Lord struck him down, and he was eaten by the worms and died. (Acts 12:23) We must glorify God in all that we do.

## I'm Praying For You

While growing up in the Mississippi Delta, our family went through hard times. We did everything that we could to make ends meet. At a young age, I remember my mother telling me not to open the door if anybody came by. She said to stay in the room and watch TV and she would be back in an hour. Then she would go into her room and close the door. My mother did this often, then one day I asked her what she was doing while she was in there. She responded, "Baby, Mama's praying." Even as a child I understood the power of prayer.

When I got into college I would call home occasionally and before we finished our conversation my mother would tell me, "I'm praying for you." She never asked me if I was praying; she just wanted me to know that she was praying. I knew about mama's prayers. During my second year of chiropractic college I hit bottom. I ran out of money and had no one to turn to. I didn't want to call home because I didn't want to disturb my mother or cause her to worry. I received a message from the registrar's office and I knew that I was going to get kicked out of school. My tuition was past due and I had not received my financial aid nor had I been approved for a work-study program.

I went to the registrar's office and as I sat there, I remembered mama's prayers. A few moments later an admissions officer passed by and saw me. She told me that she had been looking for me and asked if I had received her message. She informed me that I had received a grant, which was being held at the admissions office. The grant covered the cost of my tuition and within a short time my work-study program was approved. My financial worries were over. I couldn't wait to tell my mother the news. And when we finished our conversation she said. " I'll be praying for you."

**Holiday Inn**
**SELECT**

PRAISE

GOD !

# CHAPTER SEVEN

# Many Gifts, One Giver

### Points To Remember:

~Our gifts are constantly trying to emanate in our lives~
~God looks at the heart and not the hand; the giver and not the gift~
~One gift can produce many talents~
~Gifts profit nothing without love~

*Because of the service by which you have proved yourselves, men will praise*
*God... Thanks be to God for his indescribable gift! (II Corinthians 9:13, 15)*

When I was a child, grownups would ask us two basic questions: (1) Who are your people; and (2) What are you going to be when you grow up? As early as seven years old, I remember telling people that I wanted to be a doctor. It seemed so clear to me at the time. I did not come from a family of doctors, neither did my family know any doctors personally that may have influenced me. It was my destiny.

I came from a family of auto mechanics. Oddly enough, when I graduated from high school at age seventeen, I was preparing to become an auto mechanic. In that ten year span I learned a few things that changed the course of my life. The first thing that I learned was that I was Black. While living in a real world in the 60's, my parents thought it would be best that I learned this fact early enough and not develop unreal expectations. We lived in the Mississippi delta at the time, which was one of the worse places to be Black.

The second thing that I learned was that we were poor. I am sure that the cost of college and medical school was of great concern to my parents. Lastly, as I got older I began to realize the academic requirements of my undertaking and was not looking forward to "spending the rest of my life in school". During that ten-year span I became both discouraged and lazy. I allowed my reality to change my dream rather than my dream changing my reality.

## Never Give Up

I gave up my goal of attending Harvard medical school and becoming a doctor and enrolled instead into Hammond Area Vocational School to become an auto mechanic. The seed that had been planted at age seven was not nurtured and had remained dormant for too long. Thorns of doubt and disbelief had choked it and made it unproductive. After three days of dirt and grease at Hammond I decided that that was not the career for me. The next day, I changed my course to electronics, which was also offered at the school.

After one year I decided to join the Air Force and "do something different". This was one of the first turning points in my life. My prior education in electronics enabled me to become a communications and navigation systems specialist, where I repaired aircraft electronic equipment. I enjoyed the military life and was determined to make it my career, then something happened. I suffered a back injury while working out and my life would be changed forever.

## What God Has Authored He Intends to Finish

The back injury that I sustained left me in intense pain, which failed to respond to traditional medical care. This left me feeling frustrated and depressed. My girlfriend suggested that I visit a chiropractor. The seed of promise that was sown nearly 20 years ago was trying to emerge. Following her suggestion, a renewed interest in health care sprang forth.

Chiropractic was so new and different to me that I began to research it on my own. The first person I asked was my medical doctor and I did not get a good report. He did not like chiropractic at all. This was the same doctor who had told me that he did not think that I would ever be able to work out with weights as I had before. He also tried to discourage me by reciting that Air Force policy prohibited heavy weight training. His prognosis for my health and life was poor and his disapproval of my future was obvious.

Rather than becoming discouraged, I felt the opposite. Even though he was not speaking on behalf of the entire medical profession, I became more determined than ever to learn more about chiropractic. What satan meant for evil, God allowed me to use for good.

Within a short time, my back problem disappeared and it has never returned. I was so impressed with chiropractic that it became my new career choice. I was determined to become a chiropractor. The seed had begun to blossom. I immediately enrolled for my chiropractic prerequisite classes and became obsessed with my renewed vision. The passion that I had and still do for the profession came from what had been locked up inside of me waiting to be released. Prior to my injury, I realized that I had begun to accept my circumstances rather than change them. I was enjoying my Air Force career but there was so much more within me waiting to be delivered. I was pregnant with a promise from God that I had been carrying long enough. I had reached my due date.

## Finding Our Gift

I have always envied gifted individuals who can do many things well. It seems that they are able to accomplish everything that they set their minds to. A gifted musician may be able to play all instruments. A gifted athlete is a natural in every sport. A person with a gift for business can start with very little money and make a fortune. These individuals enjoy great success while others struggle just to maintain mediocrity. The difference is, one uses his gift and the other operates from his talent. Too often we proceed in the direction of our talents rather than our gifts. One gift can impart many talents. A single talent can provide us with a living, but it can barely provide the true necessities of life.

## The Path Less Traveled

I believe that early in our lives we cross the threshold of our destiny and fail to recognize it. This is the narrow path that few follow. Jesus directs us to "enter by the narrow gate; for wide is the gate and broad is the way that leads to destruction, and there are many who go in by it. Because narrow is the gate and difficult is the way which leads to life, and there are few who find it."

In knowing this, we should align ourselves with God early in our lives so that he will reveal his plan to us. I have seen too many people in a never-ending search of their destiny as they hold less fulfilling jobs. I have witnessed great minds at work doing menial tasks and I have seen weak-minded people trying to hold positions that were beyond the scope of their current ability. It's so easy to become frustrated when you're on the wrong path. It is true that not everyone will accomplish great things. Greatness is reserved for the chosen few who can amass the full measure of their potential.

## A Ram in the Bush

God tested Abraham's faith by telling him to sacrifice his son Isaac as a burnt offering. When they reached the place that God had directed them to go, Abraham built an altar and bound his son Isaac and laid him upon it. Then he reached out his hand and took the knife to slay his son. The angel of the LORD called out to him from heaven, "Abraham! Abraham! Do not lay a hand on the boy," he said. "Do not do anything to him. Now I know that you fear God, because you have not withheld from me your son, your only son." Abraham looked up and there in a thicket he saw a ram caught by its horns. He went over and took the ram and sacrificed it as a burnt offering instead of his son. Abraham called that place "The Lord Will Provide."

Our church was preparing for it's annual Men's day one year and amidst the many details that had to be considered we came upon a slight hurdle. The day before the event we found ourselves without a musician. There are six musicians that regularly provide the music for our services but we received the news, on our final rehearsal, that all of our musicians were out of town or had in-town emergencies. The pianist for our choir had prepared the order of service for Men's day and the program had been set, but due to a sudden death in her family, she had to go out of town.

We showed up for rehearsal and waited, hoping that one of the musicians would turn up at the last minute. We had learned all the special selections and were prepared to give them the final touch. We were waiting for that "ram in the bush." Finally, some of the guys began planning some songs "a cappella." Then the spirit moved me over to the piano. I sat down and began to play softly, "Lead Me, Guide Me."

"I am weak and I need Thy strength and power

To help me over my weakest hour;

Let me through the darkness Thy face to see,

Lead me O Lord, lead me."

This song expressed what we were feeling that day.

I am not a highly skilled pianist and had never played an entire service before this point but the Holy Spirit had positioned me where God would use me. I didn't realize it beforehand but I was the "ram in the bush." I could have kept quiet but I recognized this as the work of God. He was allowing me an opportunity to show His power through me. I accepted the challenge. I knew that I was not capable of doing this task alone but I knew that I could do all things through Christ who strengthens me. I was up until two o'clock in the morning learning the order of service and the new selections that the choir would sing the following day. The church was filled to capacity, which made me a bit nervous but that is how God does things, in great ways. The program went well as things always do, when God is in control.

It has been said that "God does not always call the qualified, He qualifies the called." My part was to accept what He had called me to do. If I had remained silent that day perhaps no one would have known the difference, and we would have missed a blessing. When we fail to share our gifts we forfeit our blessings.

## I've had Some Bad Days

*"Rejoice in our sufferings, because we know that suffering produces perseverance; perseverance, character; and character, hope. And hope does not disappoint us". (Romans 5:3-5)*

Many people have shared their early life ambitions with me and as they spoke I could see the regret in their eyes. "I was in pre-med years ago," was one comment. Another was, "I had an opportunity to travel around the world, or I used to work in theater and loved it." These are just a few of the comments that I have heard over the years. What happened? Did they just give up? Did they have some negative experiences? The truth is, everyone has had some bad days. Our lives can change drastically at a moment's notice. The reasons may vary from a debilitating injury that ends an athletic career, corporate cutbacks, a sudden divorce, or the death of a loved one. No one is immune. It is difficult to have great faith without great trials. Trials strengthen our faith. Suffering is not the end but the transition.

When going through a transition we should not just look for a way out, we should look for a way up and become determined to rise. When we come to the crossroads, we should look to the cross.

## Learn the Lessons

Life imparts experiences and the experiences provide lessons. If we are wise we will learn from the lessons and disregard the experiences. The lessons make us better while the experiences make us bitter. Experiences tell us not-to, but the lessons teach us how-to. Experiences tell us not to trust, not to love, or not to forgive. Lessons teach us how to endure, how to have hope, how to hold on and how to believe. Experiences are not meant to teach and those who learn from them lack wisdom. Lessons are what we should value most. If we don't learn the lesson the first time then we are likely to repeat the experience time and again.

## Man Can Not Live By Talent Alone

Talents are not formed without passion. Passion is the fuel that accelerates us toward greater achievement. Those who acquire passion go further than those who merely maintain an interest. I have seen so many gifted people with talent but no passion. It is not uncommon to see talented people sitting idly while waiting for their "big break". Your talent does not impress God. It is the favor of God allows you to receive His blessings. Jesus did not go where he was liked, he went where he was needed. If you want to have favor with God, go where you are needed. Look beyond the faults of others and see their needs. Begin by using your talent where you are. Start feeding people where you find them. Decide that you are going to stop complaining and start campaigning for God's favor.

## Blessed and Highly Favored

*"By the grace God has given me, I laid a foundation as an expert builder, and someone else is building on it. But each one should be careful how he builds. For no one can lay any foundation other than the one already laid, which is Jesus Christ". (I Corinthians 3:10-11)*

Jesus Christ should be the center of our being. Everything that we do should be built on this foundation. We must also be careful to build with quality materials that meet God's approval. Wealth, security, success, or fame is a weak foundation and does not meet with God's building plan.

As we progress toward attaining God's favor, we should stop trying to duplicate the programs of other people, organizations and churches. "And Jesus grew in wisdom and stature, and in favor with God and men". Luke 2:52 If we are seeking favor with God, other people's programs will not work for us. Why? Because God has a plan and a program designed for each individual. As with fashion, what looks good on some may not suit others. God equips us only with what we need to fulfill our part of His great plan. Even if we could duplicate someone else's program, we cannot duplicate their favor. That is from God. The favor of God allows all things to work together for good.

## Sow What!

*"Teach me to do your will, for you are my God; may your good Spirit lead me on level ground." (Psalms 143:10)*

One of the greatest points of confusion among believers is the principle of sowing and reaping. Simply stated, we sow the seed, God provides the increase, we reap the harvest and God gets the glory. Our part is sowing and reaping while God provides the increase and receives the glory. We can expect problems when we try to control everything ourselves.

We can determine the type of seeds that we sow, but before we sow anything we must be in line with God's will. We cannot know God's will for our lives unless we ask him.

Secondly, we must sow the seed in the field where we hope to reap the harvest. If we want more time, then sow time. If we want more friends, then sow friendship. If we want more money, then sow money. It is not sensible to sow tomatoes and expect potatoes, or to sow beans and expect greens. Thirdly, seeds are best sown where there are needs to be met. It is important that we do not sow from what we have in abundance but sow rather from what we have in need.

*"As he looked up, Jesus saw the rich putting their gifts into the temple treasury. He also saw a poor widow put in two very small copper coins. "I tell you the truth," he said, "this poor widow has put in more than all the others. All these people gave their gifts out of their wealth; but she out of her poverty put in all she had to live on." (Luke 21:1-4)*

If we have more time than money, which describes most people, we tend to give of our time. The bible tells us that, "God will meet all your needs according to his glorious riches". (Philippians 4:19) When we give out of our need, God looks at the heart and not the hand, the giver and not the gift. He will supply accordingly.

*"Do not plant your field with two kinds of seed." (Leviticus 19:19)*

You have heard the old adage, "don't put all of your eggs in one basket." The same is true for seeds. We must not sow all of our seeds in the same field. Anyone familiar with gardening or farming will advise you not to plant two different crops side by side. If you plant a row of corn next to a row of greens, the corn is stronger and to insure its survival, will rob nutrients from the surrounding soil. The greens must strive to endure with the refuse and leftovers. The corn has deprived them of their much-needed nutrients and it also blocks valuable sunlight.

For many Christians, the church is the field where we sow our seeds. We give of our time, tithes and talents to the church. In addition, we give our offerings and spiritual gifts. When we leave the church we tend to have an "I gave at the office" attitude as we encounter others with needs. When we give so much to one place, we become satisfied and complacent. Self-satisfied Christians don't strive to grow in Christ. They feel that God accepts their work at the church as sufficient. But God regards them as "lukewarm". In light of their deeds he defines them as "wretched, pitiful and poor." (Revelation 3:16)

We cannot be loyal to the things of the church and blind to the things outside the church and expect God to be pleased. Those outside the church see us as the church. We are "the light of the world" and our light should not be hidden. We must not block the "Son-light" from others. God bids us to let our "light shine before men that they may see your good deeds and praise your Father in heaven" (Matthew 5:16).

Seeds should be sown back to where they come from. Our seed comes from God. It is the remnant of the fruit that we have enjoyed. That which we have received in faith we must sow back in faith. After we have sown our seed, we have done all that we can do. Doubt, fear and worry do not make it yield an increase. Only God can provide the increase.

There are three things that are of the essence when sowing seeds, the quantity, quality and the time. It is foolish to expect that a handful of seeds will produce a generous harvest, that giving less than our best will reap God's best or that responding when it is convenient will yield a return when it is needed. If we want to reap an "in time" harvest, we must sow an "in time" seed. This simply means that we should look for opportunities to sow seeds in the time of greatest need. If we have the goodness to sow seeds in times of need, then God will return a harvest to us in the time of our need.

When we see someone with needs, we should not judge his or her character or ability but view it as an opportunity to sow our seeds. Our needs are met in accordance with their needs. We must give them our best, cheerfully and willingly. As we see Jesus in them we are giving God glory. He said in his word that, "if you have not done it for the least of these you have not done it unto me." There are two ways to benefit from our blessings. Our first benefit is when we receive them. Our second benefit is when we pass them on to someone else. If it had not been for the grace of God this person could be us.

## Last But Not Least

*When you put a seed into the ground, it doesn't grow into a plant unless it dies first. And what you put in the ground is not the plant that will grow, but only a dry little seed of wheat or whatever it is you are planting.*

(I Corinthians 15:36-37)

Lastly, be sure to stay busy and sow a variety of seeds, for you never know which will grow—perhaps they all will. The best seeds come from fruit. And the best fruit are the fruit of the Spirit. "Sow love, joy, peace, patience, kindness, goodness, faithfulness, gentleness and self-control. Against such things there is no law". (Galatians 5:22-23)

Don't be misled. Remember that you can't ignore God and get away with it. You will always reap what you sow! Those who live only to satisfy their own sinful desires will harvest the consequences of decay and death. But those who live to please the Spirit will harvest everlasting life from the Spirit. So don't get tired of doing what is good. Don't get discouraged and give up, for we will reap a harvest of blessing in due season. Whenever we have the opportunity, we should do good to everyone, especially to our Christian brothers and sisters. (Galatians 6:7-10)

It's a spiritual as well as a natural law to reap what we sow. We sow seeds and we reap a harvest. We do not reap seeds. Sow goodness and you will reap a harvest of good things. This applies to other areas as well. Every action results in a reaction. "They sow the wind and reap the whirlwind." (Hosea 8:7) If you cross your friends, you will lose their friendship. If you plant to please self, you'll reap a crop of selfishness and sorrow. If you plant to please God, you'll reap joy and everlasting life.

## It's In You

*Those who are led by the Spirit of God are sons of God. For you did not receive a spirit that makes you a slave again to fear, but you received the Spirit of sonship (adoption). And by him we cry, "Abba, Father." The Spirit himself tes-*

*tifies with our spirit that we are God's children. Now if we are children, then we are heirs—heirs of God and co-heirs with Christ, if indeed we share in his sufferings in order that we may also share in his glory.* (Romans 8:14-17)

God's gifts are constantly trying to emanate from our lives. We will suppress them if we don't understand where they are or if we don't trust that God can do more for us than we can do for ourselves. We can only claim the gifts that God has for us by going to God. If we receive a notice from the post office stating that there is a package waiting for us, we cannot go to any post office and claim our package. We can't go to the one closest to us. We have to go to the one that sent the notice. After arriving, it is not as simple as asking for our package. We must present our notice and be prepared to show some form of identification. They have to verify that we are who we say we are. The Holy Spirit checks our I. D.

Here's a bit of advice, never send someone else to claim something that is intended for you. Don't let anyone do for you what you can do for yourself. Don't let anyone pick up your boyfriend or girlfriend at the airport or allow them to take your husband or wife home because you wanted to stay at the party. Put everything aside and do it yourself. While Esau was outside preparing to serve his father's favorite meal, Jacob was inside claiming Esau's blessings. When it's time to move we must be prepared to move. We have to put satan on notice that it's time for us to claim our gifts from God. As a child of God we can possess everything that He says that we can possess.

## BIBLICAL APPLICATION

*"For I know the plans I have for you," declares the Lord, "plans to prosper you*

*and not to harm you, plans to give you hope and a future". (Jeremiah 29:11)*

If we aspire to do anything significant in our lives, we need a plan. A plan begins with a vision from God and is carried out through faith. God works in mysterious ways but He always works through faith. We are made secure in the knowledge that "God can." The failures of God's people can be traced to two common weaknesses, their lack of vision and their lack of knowledge. God will never give us a vision without also giving us provisions. Before executing God's plan we must know unquestionably that:

> *We can do all things through Christ who strengthens us. (Philippians 4:13)*
>
> *Jesus is the author and finisher of our faith. (Hebrews 12:22)*
>
> *We are fearfully and wonderfully made. (Psalms 139:14)*
>
> *Our Redeemer lives and in the end He will stand upon the earth. (Job 19:25)*
>
> *If God is for us, who can be against us? (Romans 8:31)*
>
> *Greater is He who is in us than He who is in the world. (1 John 4:4)*
>
> *Though I walk in the midst of trouble, you preserve my life. (Psalms 138:7)*
>
> *"A man's gift maketh room for him, and bringeth him before great men".*
> *(Proverbs 18:16 KJV)*

King David was the only person in the bible who was referred to as a man after God's own heart. God was pleased with David and this was made evident when God directed the prophet Samuel to anoint him king over Israel, God's people. This was the first mention of David in the bible. From the day of his anointing, the Spirit of the Lord came upon him in power. At the same time the Spirit of the Lord had departed from King Saul, and an evil spirit from the Lord tormented him. It was recommended to Saul that a search be made for someone who played the harp well to soothe him when the evil spirits besieged him. Saul approved the search and David was presented. Saul was pleased with David and chose him as his attendant and armorbearer.

Even before Samuel anointed David, God was watching him. David was a shepherd, who was well known for his shepherding skills, but this was not his calling. He used the time afforded him while tending the sheep to play the harp and sing praises unto the Lord. God was pleased with him and his skills developed. His musical talent did not lead him to pursue a career in music; this was not his calling. He kept tending the sheep and singing praises to God. Even after David began to serve Saul, he went back and forth from Saul to tend his father's sheep. All the while God was watching. David was not brought before Saul because God had interceded. David's gift made way for him and brought him into Saul's presence. David remained humble amidst growing recognition and fame. He triumphed over Goliath, the Philistine champion, and claimed victory in the name of the Lord Almighty. Whatever David attempted he accomplished successfully. God granted him success because David had a heart that pleased Him.

David was a man of many talents, which stemmed from one gift; his love for God. Regardless of his accomplishments, David kept returning to his first love. Each time David denied himself, God exalted him, until ultimately he became King of Israel.

Whatever skills we possess have been given to us by God and are to be used in His service. We should extend ourselves beyond our talent and search for our gift. If we submit our gifts to the service of God and seek Him first, He promises that all these things (which we seek) will be provided for us.

Fisher Humphreys wrote, "Love is the ultimate spiritual gift. If we have all other gifts and lack love, we have nothing; if we have love and nothing else, we have everything."

# CHAPTER EIGHT

# Possessing Your Dream

## Points To Remember:

~Dreams give us a preview of what God has in store for us~
~What God has for us is not only possible, it's "promised"~
~God intends to keep every promise that He has made to us in His word~
~Don't delay in carrying out God's commands~

*"See, the Lord your God has given you the land. Go up and take possession of it as the Lord, the God of your fathers, told you. Do not be afraid; do not be discouraged." Then all of you came to me and said, "Let us send men ahead to spy out the land for us and bring back a report"... (Deuteronomy 1:21-22)*

Have you ever been placed on hold and were forgotten. It makes you feel less important or insignificant. We will accept an apology but it doesn't clear the offense. God's people have a history of delaying His commands and attempting to restore His grace with an apology.

God gave the Israelites a green light but they insisted on sending scouts ahead to check the intersection. They had good intentions, but poor retention. They had forgotten how God had already proved Himself to them by bringing them out of an oppressive land and restoring them as His people. They had forgotten how He fed them manna from heaven. They had forgotten that God parted the Red Sea so that they could cross on dry land.

They delayed God for forty days while they spied out the land. Their delay cost them forty years. It's not wise to put God on hold. Those twenty years and older who rebelled against God in the desert, died in the desert.

Its been said, "don't put off for tomorrow what you can do today." God's presence in our lives should motivate us to take immediate action. Faith gives a forward command; it never sounds retreat. Perceived limitations within ourselves will cause us to go backwards. At every challenge the Israelites threatened to go back to Egypt. They sent spies out to see if possessing the land was possible, while God had already told them that it was promised.

## Mountain of Transfiguration

When Kim and I got married, like many young couples, we looked for a house that fit our budget. I had always wanted a hillside home overlooking the city. I grew up in Mississippi and Louisiana where the land is flat. There are no mountains and no views. The only view that we ever saw was from a window seat during take-offs and landings at the airport.

When I first moved to Phoenix, I was awestruck by its many mountains. One day, I took a drive up to South Mountain Park, which has a spectacular view overlooking the city. I arrived there in the afternoon and stayed there until well after night-fall. The view was so breathtaking that I did not want to leave. As I descended down the mountain, I had a revelation that God meets us on mountaintops. It was an unforgettable experience.

Jesus took Peter, James and John on top of a high mountain where he was transfigured before them. This mountain is not named in the Bible but has since been called the "Mountain of Transfiguration." Jesus' face shone like the sun and his clothes became as white as the light. A bright cloud enveloped them and a voice from the cloud said, "This is my Son, whom I love; with him I am well pleased. Listen to him!" (Matthew 17:5)

Peter, James and John could not grasp what was happening at the time. It was not meant for them to experience, only to witness. They would experience this for themselves later at Pentecost. We will never fully understand the magnitude of God until we have had an experience with Him. When the twelve spies returned from spying out the "Promised Land," ten reported what they had witnessed but two reported what they had experienced. When God has transfigured us, our countenance changes. As Moses came down from Mount Sinai carrying the Ten Commandments, he did not know that the skin of his face shone while he talked with God. Our view of the world changes from the vantage point of our experiences with God. Once we ascend to the summit of our experiences, our form and appearance changes.

### Where there is No Vision

God gave me a vision on the mountaintop that I was able to capture. Sometimes God gives us a glimpse of what He has in store for us, but we are unable to receive it. The greatest opponent to our faith is fear. It keeps us from realizing our dream. Fear is usually camouflaged as money problems, lack of support, not enough time or some form of opposition. Fear is a facade; we must keep trying. As often as I could, I would go up to South Mountain and look out over the city. It was usually the first place that I would take visitors when they came to Phoenix.

Before we were married, I told Kim of my passion for a home with a view, so she began scanning magazines. She remained alert as she drove through the city. As we searched for our dream home, it soon became apparent that it would remain just that—a dream. Reality began to set in when we began to see the price range of the homes that we liked. We had two major obstacles. First, everything that we liked was priced far beyond our budget, and second, my credit was terrible. I had only been out of school a few years and even though we were earning enough money to qualify for a loan, my poor credit made us a high risk. We were resigned to finding a home where we could assume the loan without qualifying.

The Bible says, "where there is no vision, the people perish." Mountaintops are places where we go to dream. Everyone's mountaintop is different. For some, it may be looking out over the city. For others, it may be taking a drive in the country. Still for others, it's spending time alone or going for a long walk. Wherever you go and your spirit is free and your mind is at peace, is your mountaintop. Problems and cares seem beneath you. This is the place where evil dare not tread, a place with green pastures and still waters. Whenever you're feeling overwhelmed or defeated, you need to go to the mountaintop and recapture your vision.

### Yes, But!

One day Kim came home telling me excitedly about a house that she had seen. She even showed me a flyer. Although there was a sign that said, "no trespassing," she said that she could not resist. She described the view as being better than any others that we had seen. As I looked at the flyer, I saw that the home had a 270-degree view and was backed by mountain preserve property. It was perfect for hiking and climbing. It seemed perfect and I could not wait to see it.

When we arrived the next day, we dared to trespass. I had to see the view. There was a long driveway that ascended gradually, followed by a slightly sharp turn leading us to the property. As we leveled off, the view was spectacular. It was better than she had described and even greater than I could have imagined. We had just seen the first glimpse of our "Promised Land."

Now the question became whose report did we believe, a poor credit report or the report from the Lord? The credit report said that we could not have it but the report from the Lord said that it was already ours.

When the 12 spies returned from scouting out the Promised Land, they gave their report. All were in agreement relative to the abundance of the land, its resources, and its wealth. The Bible refers to it as a land flowing with "milk and honey"—a rich and fertile land bearing great riches. Joshua and Caleb gave a favorable report and encouraged the people, "We should go up and take possession of the land, for we can certainly do it." (Numbers 13:30)

Verse 31 begins with *but*. The word but has a contradictory

93

connotation. But suggests that everything said before it is subject to what is said after it. But introduces the terms of the preceding statement. The majority opinion among the scouts was 10:2 against going into the land that God had promised. They saw it as a great land, but there were giants in the land. But they had fortified cities. But they devour those living in it. But we are a weak people. They forgot the most important but of all. But the Lord was with them.

Just as the Israelites responded, Kim and I made the fatal mistake of allowing doubt and fear to influence our judgment. We both agreed that it was an exceptional property *but* we came to the conclusion that it was out of our price range, even if we could qualify for a loan. We looked at other houses for several months and nothing came close to what we had seen. My mind was still on our dream house. I became discouraged and mentioned to Kim that we should pick the best of what we had seen and move on.

*Rejoice in the Lord always. I will say it again: Rejoice! Let your gentleness be evident to all. The Lord is near. Do not be anxious about anything, but in everything, by prayer and petition, with thanksgiving, present your requests to God. (Philippians 4:4-6)*

## A Second Chance

We began to get weary after months of searching and we prayed that God would direct us. Kim suggested that we go by once more to see if our dream house was still available. We stopped by the following weekend and to our amazement, it had not been sold. We pulled another flyer from the mailbox and were surprised to find that the price had been reduced significantly. It was now closer to our price range, but it would take every penny we had to meet the cost needed for a loan (if we could qualify). We immediately called our realtor and told her the good news concerning the price. She encouraged us to attempt to qualify for a loan, considering it was a "buyer's market" at the time. This meant that the sellers were really motivated to sell. There was still one great concern. Who would give us a loan?

We arranged a showing of the house with our realtor. This marked the beginning of a long frustrating process. When we arrived at the house, we spent several minutes just admiring the view before we knocked on the door. The seller's realtor greeted our realtor at the door and when she took one look at Kim and I, her face fell. She appeared upset, as if she could have been doing something better with her time. I am certain that over the past months, there were a lot lookers, with no intention of buying. She probably felt that our appointment was another disappointment. Besides, how could a young, black couple like us afford a home like this?

She did not realize, nor did we know that God had already qualified us. He found us worthy and his grace was sufficient. There was nothing that we could have done to deserve the favor that God had in store for us. We are so accustomed to working hard for everything that we receive, it was inconceivable that we could receive anything so freely.

*For the Lord God is a sun and shield; the Lord bestows favor and honor; no good thing does he withhold from those whose walk is blameless. O Lord Almighty, blessed is the man who trusts in you. (Psalms 84:11-12)*

The seller's realtor began showing us the house and then as if something inside her snapped, she turned around and refused to go any further. She told us to just look around and when we were done she would answer any questions that we might have. And with that she took a seat in the living room and proceeded to cross her legs. As we were going down the hallway, I thought, "do we owe her any money? What is her problem?" Anyway, the house itself was nothing great; it was the view that we loved. We considered the house a bonus.

The qualifying process was grueling. We had never responded to so many questions, submitted letters of explanation, provided numerous documents, and told as many lies as we did in qualifying for that loan. Finally, it came down to the last straw; they made a ridiculous last minute request that sent us through the roof. It was something minor, but Kim and I had agreed that if they wanted anything else after that, the deal was off. The next day our loan was approved. Our dream had come true.

## BIBLICAL APPLICATION

As I looked back on that experience, I can see that God was maturing us. God's ways are not our ways and His thoughts are not our thoughts. What happened to the Israelites is similar to what happens in our daily lives:
The Israelites prayed to God and He heard their cries from heaven.
God sent his people a messenger.
God strengthened their faith through signs and miracles.
God brought them out of bondage.
God removed any further threat of their enemies.
God brought them to a place to teach them his laws and commandments.
God chastened his people for their disobedience.
God brought them to the threshold of the Promised Land.
God allowed them to send spies to scout out the land and bring back a report.

God was angered because of their disobedience and lack of faith.

God punished those who brought back an unfavorable report.

God caused those who did not believe to wander in the desert for forty years.

God did not allow those who had disbelief to enter the Promised Land.

God permitted the children of the first generation into the Promised Land.

## God is Faithful

God hears every prayer and He has sent us a messenger—his Son Jesus. It is our choice to accept His message. Rather than resisting, we should be rejoicing. In light of God's promise, we insist on knowing "when." If we are not receiving what God has promised in his word, we should not focus on what God is not doing. We should center ourselves on what we are not doing. If we are faithful to do our part, God is faithful to do His.

We are reminded in Acts 1:7, "And He said to them, It is not for you to know times or seasons which the Father has put in His own authority." As we become fully prepared to receive God's blessings, our faith will uphold us. Many of those listed in the "Hall of Faith," recorded in Hebrews 11, were still living in faith when they died. They did not receive the things promised. They only saw them and welcomed them from a distance. When we receive a word from God, we should begin praising Him for His mighty acts; according to His excellent greatness!

## God is with Us

Our faith in God should be strengthened as we see signs of His presence in our lives. When David fought Goliath, he was assured of God's presence by the works that God had already done through him. God delivers us from bondage, so that we will rely on Him. Our success should confirm God's love, and attest that He is at work in our lives. Too often we allow our mountains to distract us from our mission. God is angered when we continually insist on Him proving Himself to us.

## God is Merciful

After God brings us through the storm, he calms the storm, and there is peace. God told Abraham that, "know certainly that your descendants will be strangers in a land that is not theirs, and will serve them, and they will afflict them four hundred years. And also the nation whom they serve I will judge; afterward they shall come out with great possessions." (Genesis 15:13-14) When God brings us out of bondage, He is prepared to bless us.

What we were working for is now working for us. If we were working for money, now our money is working for us. Those who were once our superiors are now our subordinates. When God brings us to the foot of Mount Sinai, it is time for us to learn of Him. It is time to learn the Ten Commandments, attend regular worship services, Bible study classes and Sunday school. One of our greatest mistakes is to believe that we do not need to attend church regularly or hear the preaching of the gospel in order to believe in God. How, then, can they call on the one they have not believed in? And how can they believe in the one of whom they have not heard? And how can they hear without someone preaching to them? Consequently, faith comes from hearing the message, and the message is heard through the word of Christ. (Romans 10:14,17)

## God is Worthy

If we don't understand where God is taking us, we will become content with bronze when He has promised us gold. A contented spirit begins to envy things of the past and is an abomination to God. Do not look back at past jobs, relationships and previous accomplishments. Our best is yet to come. Near the end of his life, internationally known architect Frank Lloyd Wright was asked, which of his works did he claim as his best? His response was "THE NEXT ONE." He believed that his best work was yet to come. We must never settle for less than our best. If we become content with less, we will be content to serve lesser gods. Furthermore, since they did not think it worthwhile to retain the knowledge of God, he gave them over to a depraved mind, to do what ought not to be done. (Romans 1:28) If we turn from God, He will leave us to our own desires. We must continually seek God's face and turn from our own lusts. To turn from God is to reject Him.

## God Delivers

Whatever God places before us, is for us! We must be able to discern when God has placed it there. Oftentimes, what we have been seeking is right before our eyes. God has placed it squarely in front of us. It appears too easy. We insist that complicated problems require complicated solutions. What God allows us to see is just a sample, a down payment, of what is to come. Our attitude is, "What I really want is a house, but all I can afford is a shack. Everywhere I go, houses are popping up before me. If I can just move some of these houses out of my way, there has got to be a shack out there somewhere. Maybe it's not my time yet. Maybe God has forgotten about me."

Sometimes, what we want is not on the way; it's actually in the way. We often have the misunderstanding that if times have been tough, they will remain tough. Don't be surprised if you find that your Promised Land is occupied or appears unattainable. If the Lord is pleased with you, he will lead you into that land, a land flowing with milk and honey, and will give it to you. "Only do not rebel against the Lord. And do not be afraid of the people of the land, because we will swallow them up. Their protection is gone, but the Lord is with us. Do not be afraid of them." (Numbers 14:8-9) The end for us is just the beginning for God.

### God Chastens

There is nothing more distasteful to God than witnesses who will not witness or believers who do not believe. The power of your testimony can restore hope to a hopeless condition, and restore light to a dark world. Doing the will of God may not always be pleasant or make us popular, but we must not hold back what the world needs for fear of retribution. If we deny Jesus before men, He will deny us before the Father. Titus 1:16 says, "they claim to know God, but by their actions they deny him. They are detestable, disobedient and unfit for doing anything good."

### God Remembers

*Then the children of Israel groaned because of the bondage, and they cried out; and their cry came up to God because of the bondage. So God heard their groaning, and God remembered His covenant with Abraham, with Isaac, and with Jacob. And God looked upon the children of Israel, and God acknowledged them. (Exodus 2:23-25)*

God remembers and keeps his covenants. It was not their groaning that God responded to, it was His covenant with Abraham and his descendants. As children of Abraham we receive the same mercy and protection. We must guard our hearts and minds through Christ Jesus.

Righteousness exalts a nation, but sin is a reproach to any people. If sin in is our hearts it will affect our judgment and will separate us from God. Being apart from God is to be without his protection. The children of Israel who were under twenty years of age were protected by God and were not held accountable for the sins of their disobedient parents. It was the faith of their forefathers that permitted them to enter the Promised Land.

Your promise from God may appear beyond your reach but it is not beyond your faith. Faith is your bridge over troubled waters. It is the shield, with which you can extinguish all the flaming arrows of the evil one. If you are faithful to follow God, obey his commands, and keep his statutes, He will send an angel ahead of you to guard you along the way and to bring you to the place He has prepared.

# CHAPTER NINE

# A Change of Character

## Points To Remember:

~Suffering builds character and character restores faith~
~Obedience is greater than sacrifice~
~The bible is full of characters and God used them all~
~Those whom God chooses, He changes~

*"I urge you to keep up your courage, because not one of you will be lost; only the ship will be destroyed".* (Acts 27:22)

When something breaks, our first inclination is to discard it. It is broken and useless. There are times when we must cling to the pieces. Logic will tell us to let them go, but something deep inside of us tells us to hold on. Whenever your dreams appear to be shattered, cling to the pieces.

The apostle Paul was a prisoner on a ship bound for Rome when the storms came. The crew struggled with the storm for 14 days and grew weary. One night an angel stood beside Paul and told him the ship would be lost but their lives would be spared. In an attempt to escape from the ship, the sailors let the lifeboat down into the sea. But Paul warned them that anyone attempting to save their lives would lose it. When daybreak came they recognized land and attempted to sail ashore. The pounding of the surf broke the battered ship into pieces. All that could, swam ashore and the rest got there on planks or on pieces of the ship. In this way everyone reached land safely.

God has a way of taking broken homes, broken marriages, broken dreams and disappointments and making them whole. What the doctors can not help, God heals. What the world rejects, God accepts. God makes the incurable, curable; the proud, humbled; the lowly, exalted; and the weak, strong.

As with Paul, we may struggle with storms on our day to day journey. But all is not lost. Though we feel shipwrecked on an island of despair, there is still hope. God told them that their ship would be lost but their lives would be spared. He was in effect telling them that He would spare their lives so that they would understand that their shipwreck was no accident. Regardless of what we have endured, our survival is no accident. God could have taken the men down with the ship but the fact that they survived meant that He was not done with them. The men valued the ship, which was used for their purpose. But God valued their lives, which were used for His purpose.

Wrapped up in each day is a new beginning, a gift of hope and life. When we value things more than life, we can be of little service because we're wrapped up in something that can be lost. God wants us to be wrapped up, tied up and tangled up in Him.

Before you wave the white flag of surrender, remember God's word, "in the world ye shall have tribulation: but be of good cheer; I have overcome the world." (John 16:33) We ask, "Lord, why didn't you come by sooner? Why did you let me struggle for so long?" We already know the answer. We would not have listened. We listen better when God has our undivided attention. Any attempt to stay in control only takes us deeper into despair.

Those whom God chooses, He changes. We possess no power of our own. God has all power in His hands. There are times when we may have received undeserved punishment and at other times undeserved praise but we must regard them both as the changes of the season. A story that I heard in a sermon expresses it best.

A farmer had to transport his birds across town, so he put them in cages and secured them on the back of his pick-up truck. The birds were perched in their cages and as the farmer increased his speed the birds began to feel the wind pass around them and instinctively they began to flap their wings. They were still bound in their cages but the temptation to fly was too compelling. It would have been best for them to just sit back and enjoy the ride. The sermon text was "Are you flapping or are you flying?"

As God is moving us through life we should learn to be still and enjoy the ride. It is a natural tendency, as we feel momentum taking place, to start flapping. The word of God tells us to be still and know that I am God. This does not mean that we should become inactive and lazy. When faced with situations that encase us, we must not despair or become discontented. Never give up or give in because in due season (the fifth season) we shall reap if we don't faint. As in the story, the birds were being transported while they were still in their cages. Sometimes while we are in our circumstances, if we stop flapping long enough we may discover that our cage is moving.

## The Character of Humility

*"If my people, who are called by my name, will humble themselves and pray and seek my face and turn from their wicked ways, then will I hear from heaven and will forgive their sin and will heal their land".* (II Chronicles 7:14)

Routinely, during our church service, our pastor will welcome back a family or member who has been away for an extended period of time. Following this announcement, what you may see and hear is a bit of whispering or comments throughout the sanctuary. What they are saying is, "I didn't know that they were gone." It is a harsh reality, but it is difficult to be missed when no one knows you are absent. It makes a statement about the power of your presence and the effectiveness of your witness. There are some people who you can feel in your spirit when they are absent. There may not be anything obvious about their presence, but you can sense it when they are absent. That is the kind of person that we should strive to model. Not the proud, self-exultant ones who walk into the room and demand attention, but the gentle, humble spirits who enter and command it.

As we think about the character of the persons we truly miss, we can conclude that the ones who are missed are the ones who are making a difference. Others may justify the weakness of their character by saying that they are not hurting anyone, but they're also not helping anyone. The bible states that they are useless. "Every tree that does not produce good fruit will be cut down and thrown into the fire." (Matthew 3:10)

Members who are missed are the ones who call to check on other members when they are absent. They visit the sick even when they themselves are not feeling well. They shoulder responsibility. They encourage others. They give of themselves. In the world this does not happen. Sick people don't think of praying for other sick people. And the hungry don't reach out to others who are hungry. They only feel obligated to the giver and only for the portion that they have received.

Those who planted the trees that produce the fruit we buy, may have already passed on. They may no longer enjoy the fruit of their labor but they still saw the need to plant the tree. As we go through our lives, we must stop to sow seeds knowing that we may never reap the harvest in our lifetime. We must do it today because tomorrow is not promised.

## Character Of Submission

*"And I, the Son of Man, have come to seek and save those like him who are lost." (Luke 19:10)*

When we come to Jesus it is often in an attitude of surrender rather than submission. Surrender means the giving up completely of something that we cherish after striving to keep it. The term surrender means that, "I can no longer maintain what I have, so at the threat of losing it all, I relinquish it." On the other hand, submission is to give in to authority or superior force. It implies voluntary, deliberate letting go. Surrender is a giving up and is the only option to defeat, whereas, submission is giving in and has no option. God directed his people to turn from their wickedness and submit to Him.

A lame man was positioned daily at the gate of the temple, called "Beautiful". The idea was that those going into the temple would have softer hearts than others and would be more prone to giving. He surrendered himself to his condition rather than submitting to God. Upon entering the temple, Peter saw the man and said, "...what I have I give you. In the name of Jesus Christ of Nazareth, walk." Taking him by the right hand, he helped him up and instantly the man's feet and ankles became strong. He jumped to his feet and began to walk. Then he went with them into the temple courts, walking and jumping, and praising God. (Acts 3:6-8)

Spiritual emptiness creates a void that cannot be filled with possessions or success. Religion cannot fill this void. Prayer cannot fill it. And confession cannot fill it. True fulfillment must begin with a relationship with Jesus Christ. We often come to Him as a last resort. Jesus is not the end, but the beginning. Our discovery of him allows us to confess our sins, acknowledge our faults and announce our blessings.

## The Character God Chooses

*"When I was a child, I talked like a child, I thought like a child, I reasoned like a child. When I became a man, I put childish ways behind me".*
(I Corinthians 13:11)

This scripture mentions childish ways, not childlike ways. There is a difference. Childlike means innocent and pure; childish is irresponsible and careless. Childish behavior that is not put away, degrades our character. It is difficult for us to face God when we cannot face ourselves.

God chose Saul as the first king of his people the Israelites.

Saul was highly favored by God and was well regarded among the people. After the prophet Samuel anointed him, he was directed to go to Gibeah. As he approached the town, he met a procession of prophets with lyres, tambourines, flutes and harps being played before them, and they were prophesying. The Spirit of the Lord came upon Saul in power and he began prophesying with them. The scripture quotes that Saul was "changed into a different person."

A further example of Saul's humility was evidenced on the day that he was to be presented before the people. When they looked for him, he was not to be found. They inquired of the Lord and the Lord told them that Saul had hidden himself among the baggage. But as Saul's power grew, so did his pride. After some time, he began to turn away from God and erected a monument in his own honor. He was told by God, "go, attack the Amalekites and totally destroy everything that belongs to them. Do not spare them; put to death men and women, children and infants, cattle and sheep, camels and donkeys." (I Samuel 15:3)

Saul disobeyed God and his reply to the prophet Samuel was, "but I did obey the Lord. I went on the mission the Lord assigned me. I completely destroyed the Amalekites and brought back Agag their king. The soldiers took sheep and cattle from the plunder, the best of what was devoted to God, in order to sacrifice them to the Lord your God at Gilgal." (I Samuel 15:20)

In verse 22 Samuel responded, "To obey is better than sacrifice, and to heed is better than the fat of rams." God is very clear on this point. He reminds his people throughout the bible that obedience in one's character is far better than sacrifice.

## BIBLICAL APPLICATION

When Jesus came to the region of Caesarea Philippi, he asked his disciples, "Who do people say the Son of Man is?" They replied, "Some say John the Baptist; others say Elijah; and still others, Jeremiah or one of the prophets."

"But what about you?" he asked. "Who do you say I am?"

Simon Peter answered, "You are the Christ, the Son of the living God."

Jesus replied, "Blessed are you, Simon son of Jonah, for this was not revealed to you by man, but by my Father in heaven. And I tell you that you are Peter, and on this rock I will build my church, and the gates of Hades will not overcome it. (Matthew 16:13-18).

If we truly wish for change to occur in our lives, our character must change. We must become cool in the summer, warm in the winter and calm in the storm. In short, we must reflect the character of Jesus. Our deeds should not be done so as to convince others that we are in Christ, they should be done so convincingly that they see Christ in us.

When Jesus asked his disciples this question, "who do people say the Son of Man is?" they replied, "some say... others say... and still others say..." This reply was based upon his reputation. The disciples was asked this question in part because of the growing multitudes that followed Jesus. Many followed Him because of His reputation as a healer and teacher but they did not know His true character. Even today there are those who follow Jesus without fully understanding who he is.

When he posed the question to his disciples, "who do you

say I am?" he wanted to verify what they had acquired from their experiences with him. They had traveled with Jesus, had gotten to know him privately and he wanted to know what they were telling the people. Peter answered saying "you are the Christ, the Son of the living God." That was the answer Jesus was in search of. He knew that Peter could not have known this unless it had been disclosed from on high.

Peter's response was made known by divine revelation. It was this foundation, this revelation, upon which the church was built. Peter was able to separate the miracles of Jesus from the Messiah, Jesus. "You are the Christ, the Messiah, the Anointed One, and the Son of the living God." The miracles did much to expand Jesus' reputation but the knowledge of Him revealed his character. Anyone, who does not know the character of Jesus, do not know Him. They are only following His reputation. Any church that is not built on this Rock, this revelation, will encounter difficulty leading others to Jesus.

After Jesus began his ministry he went to his hometown and began to teach in the synagogue. Many who heard him were amazed. "Where did this man get these things?" they asked. "What's this wisdom that has been given him, that he even does miracles! Isn't this the carpenter? Isn't this Mary's son and the brother of James, Joseph, Judas and Simon? Aren't his sisters here with us?" And they were offended by him. Jesus could not do any miracles there, except lay his hands on a few sick people and heal them. And he was amazed at their lack of faith. The scripture does not say that he did not do any miracles it clearly states that he could not because of their lack of faith. They did not know Jesus as their lord and savior; they knew him as the carpenter, Mary's son. If we do not know Jesus as our lord and savior we will forfeit the benefits of his presence. The evidence of our suffering suggests that we must know him as Mary's son, because if we knew him as our lord and savior we would experience miracle-working power.

The people at Jesus' hometown were so centered on who he was that they could not receive what he had. Many churchgoers today are still confused. How can they believe in someone that they do not know? How can they witness concerning what they have not seen?

# CHAPTER TEN

# Running When No One Is Chasing You

## Points To Remember:

~In the presence of fear we can choose power~
~Repenting is turning away from sin and turning toward God~
~After we pass a test we should share our answers~
~Jesus Christ is the same yesterday, today and forever~

*"As for those of you who are left, I will make their hearts so fearful in the lands of their enemies that the sound of a windblown leaf will put them to flight. They will run... even though no one is pursuing them."* (Leviticus 26:36)

In this verse, God threatened to bring terror upon those who rejected his decrees and violated his covenant. If they remained hostile toward him and refused to listen to him, God said that He would multiply their afflictions seven times over, as their sins deserved.

2 Timothy 1:7 tells us that, "God has not given us a spirit of fear, but of power and of love and of a sound mind." The

first point that this scripture makes clear is that fear does not come from God. The second point is that fear is a spirit. And finally, fear is a choice.

In the presence of fear we can choose power. The only power that fear possesses is the power that we surrender to it. Kim used to be dreadfully afraid of spiders. If she was looking at a magazine and saw a picture of a spider, she would throw the magazine down and scream. Finally she faced her fear and decided that she was not going to be afraid anymore. When we surrender our power to fear, in any given situation, the fear will govern how we respond. One of our most powerful weapons we have against fear is faith. Where faith abounds, fear is abated.

When facing fear we must choose "fight or flight." For many of us our first instinct is to run. When I was a child, my brothers and I were afraid of ghosts. My first experience occurred when I was about seven years old. There was a lady in our neighborhood named Mrs. Dixon who had died. We heard that some people came back as ghosts and the word was that Mrs. Dixon was back. Several of us children would be coming home late at night, then someone would yell out, "there's Mrs. Dixon." All hell would break loose and we'd run full speed and not stop until we got home. My mom would hear us running onto the porch and reprimand us saying, "don't come in here with that foolishness." Then she would look out the window. I don't think that she was too sure about Mrs. Dixon either.

There were other times when we'd be outside playing and someone would scream, "I just saw Mrs. Dixon." That was that, playtime was over. As I think back to that time, we saw Mrs. Dixon more after she died than when she was alive. Now here's the irony of it all. I never saw Mrs. Dixon. I was responding to what others said. I was running and no one was chasing me. If we listen to others long enough, their fears will become our fears. Their beliefs will become our beliefs. And their standards will become our standards. We will begin to line ourselves up with the world rather than aligning ourselves with the Word.

*God is our refuge and strength, an ever-present help in trouble. Therefore we will not fear, though the earth give way and the mountains fall into the heart of the sea, though its waters roar and foam and the mountains quake with their surging. (Psalm 46:1)*

## I've fallen and I Won't Get Up

One of our greatest fears of the ageing is the fear of falling. If you have ever watched a child fall, they do it gracefully, get up right away and keep going. Adults are awkward and clumsy. We cause ourselves more harm by trying to break our fall than just letting go. After falling, we begin looking back to see what caused it. Then we allow ourselves to become upset and insist on blaming others. We endure so much when we could just take a few lessons from our children.

The same applies to other areas of our lives. It is very discouraging to see someone with wonderful potential who has suffered a fall in their personal or professional life and they won't get up. They are still trying to figure out what happened. They are still blaming other people and are not trying to help themselves. They are angry with God for allowing it to happen and they have become content. So there they are, in the same place, still assessing the past. This is called the "paralysis of analysis." Their fear of falling again has halted any progress that they could make. If we cling to excuses and alibis as reasons why we are not accomplishing more, then we will achieve very little. Excuses become the crutches that we use to support our fears. These rationalizations are not preventing us from falling; they preclude us from rising.

## Thou Shall Have No Other Gods

*"It is a dreadful thing to fall into the hands of the living God".*
(Hebrews 10:31)

When we're not getting the result that we want from God, we should close our eyes, take a deep breath and count to ten... commandments. Beginning with "thou shalt have no other Gods before me."

Other Gods are anything or anyone that is keeping us from a right relationship with the true God. If we are too self-absorbed, agonizing about every incident that happens in our lives, we can become our own God. Repenting is not only turning away from sin but also turning toward God. If we do not accept his mercy, we will eventually face his judgment. If we love God and keep his commandments, we have nothing to fear.

*"There is no fear in love. But perfect love drives out fear, because fear has to do with punishment. The one who fears is not made perfect in love".*
(1 John 4:18)

God called his people a "stubborn and stiff-necked people" because they only looked up to him when they needed him. As a chiropractor, I have seen a lot of stiff necks, and my patients always believe that their condition "just happened." Stiff necks can be painful and pain incites fear in people. As we advance in years, our bodies naturally become stiff from misuse, disuse and abuse. But the neck is particularly vulnerable. What makes it susceptible is that when its proper alignment is not maintained a gradual shifting of its structures occurs. Over time this shifting causes tension, stiffness and pain. Looking up becomes our most restricted movement.

I recommend regular adjustments to my patients to maintain the proper alignment. If we omit regular adjustments with God, we will lose our alignment with him. Regular adjustments occur when we are continually adjusting our will to his will. Misalignments occur when we strive to adjust God's will to our own.

## Back To The Future

One of my favorite movies is Back To the Future. Here's the story of an average family with day to day struggles. The father has not realized his full potential because he had never come to the realization that he could affect his destiny. He was still being commanded by the same people and issues that he endured during high school. Through some experiment, his son is transported thirty years in the past. His ultimate goal is to meet the professor who sent him back in time and to find a way to return to the present. He also has an opportunity to meet his parents while they are still in high school. The professor warns him not to interfere with any events that he witnesses because, "it will have severe repercussions in the future." He sees how his dad allows himself to be pushed around by others and he befriends him. This relationship with his father results in his father standing up to a bully and punching him out.

Upon the son's return to the present, he is shocked at the

changes that have taken place. His father has pursued his dream of writing and has become a noted author. They are living a completely upgraded lifestyle, the bully who had harassed his father now works for him and his mother and father look younger and healthier. His father's confidence has completely permeated the entire family. His children are more productive, his wife respects him and he has established himself among his peers.

This one act of courage changed the father's life and the lives of his children. When we fail to take our proper place in the world, not only is the world deprived of our gifts, but the gifts of our offspring as well. The Bible speaks of the place of honor that one should have among the elders and in the community. We have often heard people say things like, "If I could do it all over again, I would have done it a lot differently." We cannot change our past, but we can affect our future.

What is the hidden agenda in your life that was never played out, has never been expressed for fear of rejection, or just plain fear? How many champions have there been who were never crowned? Grammy award winners who never performed? Or presidents who never ran for office? We often change when it becomes more difficult to suffer than to change. What we will inevitably find is that the change was for the better. We can begin by setting our sights toward heaven and allowing God to strengthen us. Having done this, we will emerge with such power that nothing under heaven can stop us.

### Keep It Simple

*"Jesus Christ is the same yesterday and today and forever"*. (Hebrews 13:8)

I've noticed that supermarkets will change their merchandise often and at a moment's notice. They will move items to different locations within the store in an effort to "serve us better." I have never received a call from them asking me where I would like them to place certain items or which brands I would like them to carry, but I trust that they mean well. What happens is that I will look for ketchup in the usual place and finally find it three aisles over? The little store in the neighborhood where I grew up still puts the bread in the same location where I remember and where my mother remembers it being. Some things don't change.

As we examine the world, the only thing that's constant is change. Upon closer observation, we find that few things are original. They are just revolving on an axis.

*Whatever is has already been, and what will be has been before; and God will call the past to account.* (Ecclesiastes 3:15)

Styles of the past are beginning to appear again. This is not only true with fashion but entertainment, sports, and other industries. Coming full circle is defined as a series of developments that lead back to the original position. The Bible refers to it as "wandering."

The Israelites wandered in the desert for forty years before they were allowed to enter the "Promised Land." God did not prevent them from entering; their disobedience kept them out.

In many ways, we are like the Israelites. When we are disobedient to God and do not keep his commandments, he allows us to wander. When someone has a "wandering spirit," they are constantly changing. One who wanders, also wonders excessively. They are wondering about their jobs, their children, their health, the future, what people are saying, etc.

At the close of the twentieth century, there was a lot of concern about Y2K. The stores, banks and gas stations were already crowded as people panicked in preparation for the worse. Fear of the unknown causes us to panic while fear of the known causes us to prepare. If we know and fear God, then we should be prepared at all times for his coming. If we do not know him, we will find no cause to prepare and will panic upon his return.

Wandering people are undependable. They feel controlled by their circumstances, so rather than change them they keep creating new ones. The Bible says that, we are both in authority and under authority. When we continue to relinquish our authority to those things that we should control, we lose our power.

The Israelites ate manna everyday for forty years. Some of us can't eat the same thing for two days without complaining. Meanwhile, God protected them during this entire time. Their clothes did not wear out and their ankles did not swell.

My mother and grandmother understood the value of a simple life. They rarely complained, seldom tired of anything and almost never threw anything away. They had few worries; few fears and they reverenced God. They would take clothes that had been handed down so many times that they could not be handed down anymore, then would cut them up and use them as cleaning rags or as patches for a quilt. When soap had gotten too small to use, they saved the pieces and when there were enough, they would bind them together and make their own brand. They did not receive a great inheritance that they could pass down to their children but they did leave a legacy. The legacy consists of love, joy, peace, patience, kindness, goodness, faithfulness, gentleness, and self-control.

## BIBLICAL APPLICATION

After the prophet Elijah had ordered the prophets of Baal to be slaughtered, he climbed to the top of Mount Carmel and prayed to God. At this point, there had not been any rain on the face of the earth for three and one-half years. Elijah knelt down to the ground and put his head between his knees and prayed. He asked his servant to go and look toward the sea, and when the servant returned he said, "There is nothing there." Seven times Elijah told him to go back. The seventh time the servant told him that he saw a cloud as small as a man's hand rising from the sea. Persistent prayer does not stop when there is no immediate answer. Praying more than once does not stop the petition from being granted nor does it indicate that we didn't pray in faith the first time. A true prayer warrior endures until their change comes.

Upon hearing the news about the small cloud, Elijah knew that the rains were at hand. As we look out over our horizon, we should rejoice when we see a small "cloud of a blessing" coming our way. This means that God is about to pour out blessings upon us. The power of God came upon Elijah so strongly that he girded up his clothes and tucked them into his belt and ran six miles, surpassing those riding chariots, to Jezreel.

When he heard that Jezebel was intent on having him killed for having her prophets executed, he was afraid and ran for his life. He went a day's journey into the desert and asked God to take his life. This is the same prophet that had just witnessed God perform two great miracles through him, but he was still afraid.

When God finally spoke to Elijah, he asked him this question, "What are you doing here, Elijah?" God is asking us the same question, "What are you doing here?" The Lord instructed him to go and stand on Mount Horeb in his presence and He would pass by. God sent a powerful wind that tore the mountains apart, but the Lord was not in the wind. After the wind, he sent an earthquake, but the Lord was not in the earthquake. After the earthquake, came a fire but the Lord was not in the fire. God had sent three powerful forces to Elijah to demonstrate his awesome presence but did not choose to speak through any of them. After the fire, came a gentle whisper, then the Lord repeated his question, "What are you doing here, Elijah?" God had sent "Earth, Wind and Fire," but he did not need them to speak to his prophet. Neither does God need them to speak to us. When we are afraid we must learn to be still and listen for the gentle whisper.

## Go Back Where You Came From

*"For as many as are led by the Spirit of God, these are sons of God. For you did not receive the spirit of bondage again to fear, but you received the Spirit of adoption by whom we cry out, "Abba, Father." (Romans 8:14-15)*

Sometimes our efforts to resolve present fears are perfected by facing our past. Previous faults, mistakes and frailties are replayed when we consider new challenges, and we are left feeling inadequate. We will never succeed at running from our past, because it is not behind us, it is within us. Everywhere we go, we carry them. If we are controlled by our past, there exists weaknesses in our character or personality, which must be confronted and overcome. A chain is only as strong as its weakest link.

If we are slaves to our past, we will become people pleasing rather than God-pleasing. Even Christians try to conceal their past for fear that those around them will misjudge or condemn them. When we confess our sins and accept Christ as our personal savior, our sins are forgiven. We are not sin-less, we have become sin-cere. This means that we are free from sin, not free to sin. The sins and bondage of the past no longer bind us; we are now lead by the Spirit of God. All of our efforts, from this point, will be made with a sincere heart, seeking God's truth and guidance.

God often sends those whom he chooses, back to their past. He will make us face the fear that we have been avoiding. God sent Jacob back to face Esau. He sent Moses back to Egypt. He sent Jonah back to Nineveh. He sent Elijah back to Jezreel. When we have conquered fear, it shows that we have learned to rely on God.

## Tell Your Story

When we have overcome our fears, we must be mindful to share our testimonies. There are others who are going through the same thing that we have been through and they need encouragement. We should also share our story with our children. We should not be embarrassed by our past but rather we should embrace it. Our stories should tell of how God has brought us through. We must tell our children that God was the bridge that brought us over because they will need to use that same bridge some day. By sharing our experiences with our children, they won't have to make the same mistakes that we made. Some of our children are searching for something, but they do not know where to find it. They are lost in a whirlwind of bewilderment. We must teach them to humble themselves and pray, seek God's face and turn from wickedness. And surely if they continue to pray and not grow weary, then God will provide and He will prevail.

# CHAPTER ELEVEN

# Fullness of Power

### Points To Remember:

~A lamp cannot give forth light until it receives power~
~If we desire the best, we will pay the full price~
~If we trust and never doubt, God will surely bring us out~
~Life and death is in the power of the tongue~

*From the fullness of His grace we have received one blessing after another.*
(John 1:16)

God told Abram, "know for certain that your descendants will be strangers in a country not their own, and they will be enslaved and mistreated four hundred years. But I will punish the nation they serve as slaves, and afterward they will come out with great possessions." (Genesis 15:13-14) Whenever God's people endure persecution or suffering, God will greatly reward them as He delivers them.

The last plague that God brought upon Egypt, prior to the

exodus of His people, was the death of all their firstborn. At midnight God passed over Egypt and every Egyptian household suffered death. The Egyptians urged the Israelites to hurry and leave their country, for they feared that God would kill them all. "The Israelites did as Moses instructed and asked the Egyptians for articles of silver and gold and for clothing. The Lord had made the Egyptians favorably disposed toward the people, and they gave them what they asked for; so they plundered the Egyptians." (Exodus 12:35-36)

Acquiring the "fullness of God's power" is the optimum hope of our existence. It is being whole, (mind, body and spirit). One who operates in the fullness of power maintains the highest standard in all areas of his or her life. When we are in Christ and remain connected to Him, He becomes our continuous source of power. Just as our homes are linked to a power source, the same should be true of our lives. Each room in our house is connected to a main power source. If we measured the power outlet in our bathroom, it is the same as the bedroom or at any other area. Our house is designed to operate in the fullness of power at every location.

Before anything can function it must be connected to a power source. A lamp was designed for one specific purpose, to give forth light. It may be decorative or have other intrinsic value but it does not accomplish it's intended purpose until it disperses light. But before it can fulfill it's mission it must receive power.

We cannot carry out the work that God has ordained us to do until we receive His power. When we abide in Christ and allow Him to abide in us, we receive his power. It is not just present in part of our life, it is present in all areas of our life. As with our homes, power is present in each room but we still have to make the connection, before we can receive it. If there is a room that is without power, it does not mean that power is not available, it only means that we have not made a connection with that room and the source of power. If we want God to supply power to all areas of our lives, we have to connect with Him in each area. If we want to receive God's power in our finances, jobs, relationships, and health, we have to avail those areas to Him.

## Making The Connection

Making the Christ—connection occurs in our finances when we remember where the power to get wealth comes from. Our reasonable service is to tithe a portion of our income back to the storehouse (church). This connection happens on our jobs when we take a few minutes during the day to study God's word. We connect with God in our relationships when we attend worship services together, pray together and study God's word together. A common mistake we make in our personal relationships is we may seek a mate, expecting that they will meet all of our needs. These types of relationships rarely last because there is no one thing, outside of Christ, that can produce sufficient power to sustain us in the fullness of joy, peace, happiness and love. We unfairly place the burden on others to meet these needs, which is impossible.

"(Only) God will meet all your needs according to his glorious riches in Christ Jesus." (Philippians 4:19) We cannot give that which we have not received. We are only capable of giving the full measure of love when we have received it. If we are in constant supply or have an abundance of love we are able to give it freely. True love gives without expectation and receives without obligation. There must be a source of love for it to exist within us.

## Just Enough

*"For in Christ all the fullness of the Deity lives in bodily form, and you have been given fullness in Christ, who is the head over every power and authority".*
(*Colossians* 2:9-10)

Too often we operate in sufficiency rather than in fullness. We settle for barely enough, while God promises us more than enough. It was common many years ago for some homes to not have electricity. People relied on batteries, kerosene lamps and candles, which was costly and inconvenient. The quality of life was sufficient but it was not full. Jesus said, "I have come that they may have life, and have it to the full." (John 10:10) We can only have fullness in Christ. Outside of Him we tend to seek temporary fill-ups. We fill ourselves with alcohol, drugs and excess but they only bring short-term pleasure and long-term pain.

Even today, when we temporarily lose power in our homes, our first instinct is to check our surroundings. If there is a power outage in neighboring homes, we may become complacent because we feel that it is not our responsibility. Those without power often fail to report it because the assumption is someone else will. The same applies to life. If we perceive a loss of power or feel powerless, we tend to verify that this is common to those around us. We have become too comfortable around powerless people. We more willingly expend time talking about our mountains than talking to them.

The proper thing to do during a power outage is to contact the power company and schedule a service call. In powerless situations the bible tells us, "Don't worry about anything; instead, pray about everything. Tell God what you need, and thank him for all he has done. If you do this, you will experience God's peace, which is far more wonderful than the human mind can understand. His peace will guard your hearts and minds as you live in Christ Jesus." (Philippians 4:6, 7) God is our power station and in Him we have power beyond measure.

### Sickness

As the Israelites traveled through the wilderness, one of God's rewards to them for their obedience was that he would take away their sickness. He promised them that none would miscarry or be barren and he would give them a full life span.

On a Trinity Broadcasting Network (TBN) telecast I was asked for my viewpoint regarding sickness, and my response seemed to cause quite a stir. I shared my belief that sickness is a state of the mind rather than a state of health. The host's response was, "wait a minute, you're telling me that if I'm sick, it's all in my mind?" I supported my statement with scripture. The bible tells us that, "as a man thinks, so is he". (Proverbs 23:7) Our thoughts determine what we say and do. The bible further states in Proverbs 18:21 that, "Life and death is in the power of the tongue." One who conceives sickness in his or her mind speaks it and soon embodies it. How often have you said, "I feel like I'm coming down with something," and received what you prophesied?

The term "sick" is overused in our society and describes everything from having a fever, sore throat, common cold or allergies. Even on our jobs we are allowed sick days, sick pay and sick leave. There is little consideration given for being well. It would make more sense if employers would offer incentives to departments that have the most well days. The bible does not refer to minor conditions as we relate to them today as a sickness. John 5:3 offers a category of the sick, "In these lay a great multitude of sick people, blind, lame, paralyzed, waiting for the moving of the water." These were permanent conditions. There are no biblical references to the sick having common colds and allergies.

## Don't Name It and Don't Claim It

The policy in our household regarding sickness is "don't name it and don't claim it." The usual response when someone has symptoms is to go to the doctor to find out what they have. With most sick people, I have discovered that they don't have the condition, the condition has them. In our home, we begin rebuking the spirit of sickness as soon as it tries to enter our body. We have learned that before we take a condition to the doctor, we take it to the Lord in prayer. We don't want to identify the condition because we only name and claim those things that we intend on keeping. Whatever it is that is trying to afflict us is unwelcome and we are unwilling to accept it. Return to sender.

By the blood and power of Jesus Christ we have authority over sickness. We say to the mountain go and it must go. Jesus told his disciples, "if you have faith as a mustard seed, you will say to this mountain, 'Move from here to there,' and it will move; and nothing will be impossible for you." (Matthew 17:20) He who has faith does not complain or talk about his mountain, he talks to his mountain. If we trust and never doubt, God will surely bring us out.

## We're Not Getting Older, We're Getting Better

On the night that he was betrayed, Jesus told his disciples, "Watch and pray so that you will not fall into temptation." He went off to pray but when he returned to his disciples he found them sleeping. Three times Jesus returned to find his disciples sleeping, because their eyes were heavy. Jesus responded, "the spirit is willing, but the body is weak." (Mark 14:38)

The body and mind tends to weaken over increasing years but the Spirit is made to become stronger. As we grow older, we grow in God's grace. What we lose in eyesight, God restores as insight. What we lack in education, God reveals through revelation. We are meant to become mighty in Spirit as we advance in years. Bringing our minds and bodies into subjection of the Spirit allows us to move from self will to God's will. Moses was one hundred and twenty years old when he died, yet his eyes were not dim nor his strength gone. Moses' appearance reflected his years, but his spirit reflected his youth.

Even today, God uses ordinary people to accomplish extraordinary victories. In California, a seventy-one-year-old man who sought a new hobby unveiled an amazing gift. He stepped up to the foul line in a local gymnasium and sank 2,750 free throws in a row, shattering the previous record by 700. He walked away without a miss. This amazing feat took twelve hours to accomplish and he is now listed as the greatest free throw shooter of all time.

So, what's his secret? "Focus and concentration," says Dr. Tom Amberry, a retired podiatrist. "When I'm shooting a free throw, I don't think of anything else. I am one hundred percent positive I will make the basket. I never have a negative thought on the free throw line." Winning does not surprise winners, nor does losing surprise losers. Dr. Amberry is a winner.

## My Greatest Investment

When I opened my practice, I worked many hours six days per week. This did not allow much free time. I began attending church regularly and I knew that I could do better. I was not tithing my income, I was distracted and unproductive while at work and was dealing with other petty issues. The first commitment that I made was a pledge to God that I would give fifty dollars per week in the church offering. Secondly I vowed to bring my bible to work and devote a few minutes at intervals during the day toward building a better relationship with Him. The last commitment I made was to focus my attention on my work while I was there. This is called "present time consciousness." What I was doing was creating a balance of the Spirit, mind and body as I worked. I could feel myself become unified as I began to operate at a higher level of consciousness.

Shortly after I began fulfilling my fifty dollars per week pledge I met Kim. She has been the most instrumental person in my life and my best friend since that time. If God allowed this to happen to me from giving fifty dollars per week, what would he have done if I had given one hundred dollars per week? I tease my wife with this thought from time to time. As I instituted devotion time within my daily schedule, my business began to grow. Within one year I was able to change my work schedule from six days per week to three days per week, with no significant loss of income. There have been many other things that have developed in my life since I discovered the need to incorporate God into all areas.

## Will Thou Be Made Whole?

My goal when I began private practice was to cure the world. I desired to restore every patient to the fullness of his or her potential. I found that they had a different goal in mind. They were determined to get rid of their pain, and then to get rid of me. They only wanted to become better. Once their pain was tolerable or significantly reduced they would not return until it became almost unbearable.

When Jesus healed someone, he often asked them, "will thou be made whole?" He wanted to know where their faith was. He was not interested in relief of their symptoms. Being "made whole" meant being free from infirmity. God does not provide partial cures. He is the God of completion and abundance. Jesus never gave partial sight to the blind or caused the lame to limp. His healing required no recovery period. He said, "take up thy bed and walk".

If we are not willing to accept all that God has for us, we limit His effectiveness in our lives. We sometimes want God to provide for us that which we are unwilling to provide for ourselves. We want him to change our lives, but we are not willing to change how we are living. We cannot have our complete healing without having complete faith. God wants us to bring Him the whole person, not just the broken part.

## Spiritual Authority

*"When Jesus finished saying these things, the crowds were amazed at his teaching, because he taught as one who had authority, and not as their teachers of the law." (Matthew 7:28-29)*

God instructed Moses to go and tell Pharaoh, "let my people go." Moses asked God, "Who am I, that I should go to Pharaoh and bring the Israelites out of Egypt?" Moses did not understand that when God commissioned him, he would never leave him nor forsake him. So often we respond the same as Moses when God calls us. Our reaction is "great mission God; wrong missionary."

I spoke to a friend who was struggling with her assignment as the praise and worship team leader, given to her by her pastor. She had become frustrated with some of the members of the team, because they were challenging her authority and resisted any changes that she suggested. She prayed to God about her frustration and told Him that she accepted the challenge that had been set before her. That week she came to her praise and worship choir rehearsal with a new attitude. She was no longer frustrated because she knew that God had given her the authority to do what he had called her to do. She said that she voiced her opinion of what changes will be made and invited those that could not live with the conditions set forth to leave. She said that they gave her overwhelming support and they have not questioned her authority since.

Our inclination to fill needs should not be based upon our qualifications, but on our anointing. Having the qualifications and desire does not make us effective. Our anointing prepares us for the challenge, but even after we have been anointed, we must accept the challenge. After we have accepted the challenge, we are given the authority over all opposition. This occurs in all walks of life. One person may want to be married but not be willing to accept the challenge of being a husband or wife. Another may want to have children but is not willing to accept the challenge of parenting. Too often we want to be out front but we are not willing to lead. This attitude does not glorify God. In order to be fully effective in our assigned task, we must be "in charge" of it. Being in charge of what God requires of us does not come without its price. Expect Satan to attack us, our friends to turn away, and our family to forsake us. There is a cost of doing business and we must "pay the cost if we want to be the boss".

## If You Have To Ask the Price

*"You are not your own? For you were bought at a great price; therefore glorify God in your body and in your spirit, which are God's."*
(I Corinthians 6:19-20)

A common axiom implies, if you have to ask the price, you probably can't afford it. When we ask how much something costs, is it a question of faith? Asking for the price is one way of measuring our ability to afford it. If we feel that we can't afford it we tend to wait for a sale or markdown. When we return, we often find that it's too late. We forfeit so much because we do not stand on the word of God.

Everything belongs to God. The gold and silver are His. The cattle on a thousand hills are His and all these things are ours to claim. We must claim them in His name and according to His purpose. God intends for us to have an abundant life. His Word tells us in Mark 11:24, "whatever you ask for in prayer, believe that you have received it, and it will be yours." God intends for us to have the very best. This was demonstrated when He gave the world His best, His only son, Jesus. I have found that the best never goes on sale because it is always in demand. An item is discounted when it is superseded by something better. If we want the best, then we must be prepared to give our best. When we are prepared to receive the best, we will gladly pay the full price.

## Accepting The Challenge

I struggled with my call to ministry for years, because I was unwilling to accept the challenge that God had set before me. I fulfilled various assignments of ministry within the church, such as Sunday school assistant superintendent, Lay organization president, usher, steward, choir member, etc. which I thought was enough. I did not understand that ministry extends beyond the walls of the church. Jesus spent more time ministering outside of the temple than within it. The church duties that we perform allow us to have control. If at any time we no longer have the time or desire to serve, we have the option to quit. Accepting the call to ministry is different, it means accepting the challenges that God would place before us. This is an awesome responsibility. God gives us no way out. The only option to doing God's work is death. Jonah accepted his call to ministry but he did not accept God's challenge for him to go to Nineveh. This resulted in him running away from God, endangering his own life and the lives of others. Ultimately Jonah yielded to God's call.

If we accept an assignment from God without accepting the challenge, we will eventually distance ourselves from Him and lessen the effectiveness of the mission. God commissions us to carry out a mission. As God commissions us, he confers upon us the power to accomplish our portion of the Great Commission. Our thinking as a Christian should be, we're not free until everyone is free. And we're not saved until all is saved." If every officer within the church would accept the challenges of their work, and perform their duties as if they were doing them unto God, the church mission would prosper in every way possible.

Accepting the challenges of your work, family, and calling will bring blessings upon your job, home and the world. When we accept God's challenges, we are required to give more and sometimes accept less as we are drawn closer to Him. If Jonah had not gone to Nineveh, he would have spent the rest of his life running from God. We grow stronger for our challenges, during challenging times.

## Challenges for life

At one of our children's births, Kim was in the final stages of labor when the phone rang. It was for her. A member of our birth team answered the phone and took the message. A friend was calling to inquire if she had had the baby. Kim, who was deep in labor, never knew that she had a call. After the birth, she was in the bathroom where she answered the phone when it rang. It was our pastor; he wanted to know if the baby had arrived yet. "Yes it has, it's a boy!" Kim responded cheerfully. "When was he born?" the pastor asked. "Twenty minutes ago" she replied. "Twenty minutes ago?" he asked surprisingly, "why are you answering the phone?"

What he was asking was why was she so alert, coherent and energized after going through such an exhausting experience? The answer was that God had brought her through it. She had faithfully prepared her mind, body and spirit to accept the challenge set before her. Accepting God's challenge always brings forth renewed hope and life.

## The End Result

*"I am leaving you with a gift—peace of mind and heart. And the peace I give isn't like the peace the world gives. So don't be troubled or afraid."*
(John 14:27)

As a nation we define peace as not being involved in armed conflict. The absence of war against other nations does not signify peace. It does not negate the battle that is fought on our city streets. Easy access to guns and drugs has disturbed our peace and is destroying the lives of our children. War is war regardless of the battleground or the parties involved. The cost of living has escalated over the years, but for our children, the chance of living has declined. We must have peace. But peace will not come without a price.

The bible speaks of a time of peace when lions and lambs will lie down together, the cow will feed with the bear, the infant will play near the hole of the cobra, and they will neither harm nor destroy. How is this possible? The Lord Almighty will dwell there on His Holy Mountain. Revelation 20:1-3 responds, "I saw an angel coming down out of heaven, having the key to the Abyss and holding in his hand a great chain. He seized the dragon, that ancient serpent, who is the devil, or satan, and bound him for a thousand years. He threw him into the Abyss, and locked and sealed it over him, to keep him from deceiving the nations anymore until the thousand years were ended."

This thousand-year period is referred to as the "Millennium

of Peace." Satan will be bound in a bottomless pit and Christ will rule on the earth. While satan is bound he will not be able to deceive, defraud or destroy. When his presence is banished, the very nature of all existence will change. The bible says that the lion will eat straw like the ox. (Isaiah 11:7) This sounds impractical because lions are carnivores. But they will sooner live in harmony, than kill and eat.

If we desire true peace we must bind satan and allow God to rule in our lives. We must wage war on the presence of evil, the world over. And we must take back everything that satan has stolen. War is never easy but peace is worth fighting for. In Jesus' words, "from the days of John the Baptist until now the kingdom of heaven suffers violence, and the violent take it by force."

## BIBLICAL APPLICATION

*"Therefore go and make disciples of all nations, baptizing them in the name of the Father and of the Son and of the Holy Spirit, and teaching them to obey everything I have commanded you. And surely I am with you always, to the very end of the age." (Matthew 28:19)*

Jesus' last conversation with his disciples occurred forty days after his resurrection. He spoke with them about the kingdom of God. He commanded them not to leave Jerusalem, but wait for the gift promised by his Father in heaven. He was speaking of a new baptism, not with water but with fire.

Fire will either purify or destroy. It will consume or consecrate. This depends on whether we are in the fire or the fire is in us. Jesus spoke of sending a comforter that can only be worn on the hearts of men. If we have a burning desire for worldly things, we will become consumed by evil and our suffering will not end until our flesh is destroyed. But if we have an internal (Holy Ghost) fire, it will purify our flesh and cleanse us from all unrighteousness.

Peter, a disciple of Jesus, stood outside the judgement hall while Jesus was being tried and he took the opportunity to warm himself by the fire. He found himself in the company of those who had sentenced Jesus to death. As Peter warmed his flesh, his spirit waxed cold. He knew that he could remain there as long as he denied that he knew Jesus. Whenever we are warming ourselves by satisfying our flesh we are in a position where we will either confess or deny Jesus. It is better to have cold hands and a warm heart than warm hands and a cold heart.

Jesus told his disciples that when the Holy Spirit comes upon them, they would receive power. When the day of Pentecost came, they were all together in one place. Suddenly a sound like the blowing of a violent wind came from heaven and filled the whole house where they were sitting. They saw what seemed to be tongues of fire that separated and came to rest on each of them. All of them were filled with the Holy Spirit and began to speak in other tongues as the Spirit enabled them. The power that they received enabled them to witness to those that were assembled in Jerusalem during Pentecost.

On this day, the same Peter that had denied Jesus spoke boldly to the world assembly as the Holy Spirit directed him. He verified the crucifixion and resurrection of Jesus and assured them that God had raised Jesus to life and he sits on the right hand of God Almighty. He further warned them of the perilous times that would come before the glorious return of the Lord and offered them the way to salvation.

Upon hearing this, those that were assembled asked, What must we do (to be saved)?

At that time, Peter extended the invitation to the world.

# Invitation

*"That if you confess with your mouth, "Jesus is Lord," and believe in your heart that God raised him from the dead, you will be saved." (Romans 10:9)*

A son came to his father and asked for his inheritance. After receiving his portion he strayed from home, squandered his wealth in wild living and soon lost everything. He became a hired servant and found himself feeding swine and longing for what they were eating. Then the scripture says, "he came to himself." He realized that many of his father's servants had food to spare, and there he was starving to death. Immediately he set out to go back to his father and ask for forgiveness and tell him that he was no longer worthy to be called his son. "But while he was still a long way off, his father saw him and was filled with compassion for him; he ran to his son, threw his arms around him and kissed him." (Luke 15:20)

The father had a feast prepared in his son's honor and they

began to celebrate. The father celebrated because his son was presumed to have been dead but now he was alive; he was lost but now he was found. In the same way, our heavenly Father celebrates when we come home. It doesn't matter what we have done or what we have been through, God is patient and He rejoices when we are reconciled with Him.

*I stand at the door and knock. If anyone hears my voice and opens the door, I will come in and eat with him, and he with me. (Revelation 3:20)*

Those who attend regular worship services are familiar with the invitation to Christian discipleship. It is a time for those who border on uncertainty to become certain. It's time for the wicked to cease from trouble and the weary to be at rest. It's decision time. I have shared my testimony, joy and pain with you, with hopes that you may be strengthened in your season. We may never meet but now is your opportunity to meet and come to know Jesus Christ as your personal Savior.

God's people were in bondage four hundred years before He heard their cry and remembered them. He saw that it was time to deliver them from their oppression and bring them home. Before God brought them out of Egypt, He eliminated all doubt that He was the sovereign God. He continually hardened Pharaoh's heart until in utter frustration he told the Israelites to "Go, worship the Lord." They crossed the Red Sea and rather than entering the Promised Land, they found themselves down in the valley.

They may have felt that crossing the Red Sea was a direct route to the Promised Land but they were mistaken. They still had one more river to cross. They had to spend some time in the wilderness before they could enjoy the fruits of the land sworn to their forefathers. Because of their disobedience their inheritance would be extended more than forty years. Their problem was they were prepared to receive the promise but they were unprepared to possess the land. We are only capable of possessing that which we can bear. If we are faced with a problem or trial God already knows it. It is not necessary to continually remind Him of what He already knows. He is telling us that we must bear it. His word declares that "God is faithful; he will not let you be tempted beyond what you can bear." (I Corinthians 10:13) Our trials come so that we may become stronger.

The Israelites had to be strengthened, taught to serve and learn the ways of God before they could possess the land. God led them, protected them and provided for them along their journey. As they were prepared to cross over the Jordan River, God commanded Joshua to encourage the people to be strong and courageous. They were not to be terrified or discouraged, for the Lord their God would be with them wherever they went.

After they crossed over the Jordan River, they camped to celebrate the Passover. They had not yet received the promise but they celebrated because they had made it to the Promised Land. The day after their celebration, the manna that they had eaten for the forty-year period stopped flowing and they began to partake in the riches of the land. The difference between this generation and the previous generation was when the previous generation crossed the Red Sea they camped and rather than celebrate; they began to complain. This displeased God and He did not allow any of them to enter the Promised Land.

Take note that the manna did not cease until the celebration began. You have cause to celebrate because you have made it this far. You've survived the wilderness and now you stand at the bank of the Jordan River. It's time to cross over. You may ask, "How do I know that the time is right?" If you know that things have got to get better, the time is right. If you lie down weary and wake up weary, the time is right. If you've been unsuccessful at doing things your way, the time is right. If you're tired of eating manna, the time is right.

## How Do I Cross Over?

Pray this simple prayer aloud:

Lord God Almighty, I confess my sins and ask for your forgiveness. I believe in my heart that Jesus Christ is Lord whom you raised from the dead and I accept him as my personal savior. Then all the people said "Amen" and "Praise the Lord."

# BECAUSE
# TOMORROW
## IS NOT
# PROMISED